GLOBETROTTER™

Travel Guide

TANZANIA

GRAHAM MERCER

NH

NEW HOLLAND

G733.
06651
2009

NEW
HOLLAND

*** Highly recommended
** Recommended
* See if you can

Fourth edition published in 2009
by New Holland Publishers (UK) Ltd
London • Cape Town • Sydney • Auckland
10 9 8 7 6 5 4 3 2 1
website: www.newhollandpublishers.com

Garfield House, 86 Edgware Road
London W2 2EA, United Kingdom

80 McKenzie Street
Cape Town 8001, South Africa

Unit 1, 66 Gibbes Street
Chatswood, NSW 2067, Australia

218 Lake Road, Northcote,
Auckland, New Zealand

Distributed in the USA by
The Globe Pequot Press, Connecticut

Copyright © 2009 in text: Graham Mercer
Copyright © 2009 in maps: Globetrotter Travel Maps
Copyright © 2009 in photographs:
Individual photographers as credited (right)
Copyright © 2009 New Holland Publishers (UK) Ltd

ISBN 978 1 84773 312 2

This guidebook has been written by independent
authors and updaters. The information therein represents their impartial opinion, and neither they nor the
publishers accept payment in return for including in
the book or writing more favourable reviews of any
of the establishments. Whilst every effort has been
made to ensure that this guidebook is as accurate
and up to date as possible, please be aware that the
facts quoted are subject to change, particularly the
price of food, transport and accommodation. The
Publisher accepts no responsibility or liability for any
loss, injury or inconvenience incurred by readers or
travellers using this guide.

Keep us Current
Information in travel guides is apt to change, which
is why we regularly update our guides. We'd be
grateful to receive feedback if you've noted something we should include in our updates. If you
have new information, please share it with us by
writing to the Publishing Manager, Globetrotter, at
the office nearest to you (addresses on this page).
The most significant contribution to each new edition will receive a free copy of the updated guide.

Publishing Manager: Thea Grobbelaar
DTP Cartographic Manager: Genené Hart
Editors: Carla Zietsman, Nicky Steenkamp,
Melany McCallum, Donald Reid
Design and DTP: Nicole Bannister,
Lellyn Creamer, Sonya Cupido
Cartographers: Luyolo Ndlotyeni,
Marisa Roman, William Smuts

Reproduction by Hirt & Carter (Pty) Ltd, Cape Town
Printed and bound by Times Offset (M) Sdn. Bhd.,
Malaysia

Dedication:
To my father, who gave me my love of wildlife
and travel, and to my mother, who believed in me.

Photographic Credits:
Peter Blackwell/IOA, all photographs except the
following: **Nigel J. Dennis/DD Photography**, page
103; **Martin Edge**, pages 49–54; **Corrie Hansen**,
page 118; **Graham Mercer**, pages 24, 32, 33;
Peter Ribton/IOA, pages 19, 28, 31, 35, 36, 37,
38, 44, 67; **Ariadne van Zandbergen/Africa
Imagery**, cover. [IOA = Images of Africa.]

Acknowledgements:
I would like to thank Mohamed Amin, Ms Patricia
Barrett, Ms Jamila Sumra, Ms Louise Whittle,
Gemini, of Emslies Travels, all the lovely people at
New Holland Publishing, the International School
of Tanganyika, my long-suffering safari partners
(Kevin Bartlett, Hamid Bharmal, John Boyce, Arshad
Hussain, Barry Whitemore and my wife Anjum) and
all the various rangers and game scouts of the
Tanzanian National Parks and Game Reserves.

Front Cover: *Wildebeest crossing the Mara River.*
Title Page: *Fishing boat on Zanzibar's east coast.*

CONTENTS

1. Introducing Tanzania

Tanzania, despite a wealth of natural resources, is among the world's poorest countries, and at times among its most exasperating. For visitors it can often be expensive, hot and unsophisticated. But there can be few countries in the world which are more exciting.

Its scenery alone, from the high snows of **Kilimanjaro** to the coral sands of **Zanzibar**, is splendid. And yet these landscapes are little more than stages for a whole cast of wildlife spectaculars, including the greatest of natural double-acts, **Ngorongoro** and the **Serengeti**, scene of the annual migration which involves more than two million animals.

Also in the north is Lake **Manyara**, famous for flamingoes and tree-climbing lions, and **Tarangire**, whilst in the south lie the no less exciting wildernesses of **Ruaha** and the **Selous**. Westwards, bordering **Lake Tanganyika**, rise the mountains of **Mahale** and **Gombe** chimpanzee havens, with the remote, land-locked and little-visited sanctuary of **Katavi** nearby.

Tanzania's people, generally friendly and welcoming without being servile, range from Maasai pastoralists armed with spears to cosmopolitan city dwellers. Their history begins with man's first footsteps, printed in volcanic ash millions of years ago, and extends to the present day through the remarkable Swahili civilization, the slave trade, the Zanzibari sultanate and the great age of exploration, when men such as Livingstone and Stanley strode the land.

For those who can rise above its various challenges, Tanzania, the 'real Africa', awaits with an extended arm and a ready *Karibuni!* – 'Welcome!'

TOP ATTRACTIONS

*** Serengeti National Park: spectacular animal migration.
*** Ngorongoro Crater: Noah's Ark shipwrecked in a volcanic bowl.
*** Selous Game Reserve: huge wilderness.
*** Ruaha National Park: another wonderful wilderness.
*** Mount Kilimanjaro: highest mountain in Africa.
*** Zanzibar: history, diving, fine beaches.
** Tarangire National Park: huge herds of elephant, abundant wildlife in the dry season.
** Lake Manyara: elephants, birds, striking scenery.

Opposite: *Ol Doinyo Lengai, in Tanzania's sector of the Rift Valley.*

- Visible from space, stretching from Jordan to the Zambezi, and more than 9700km (6000 miles) long, the Rift is Tanzania's main geographical feature.
- It has been formed by the intense underground stresses caused by shifts in the Earth's tectonic plates over a period of 20 million years. Even today there is turbulence below ground.
- For much of its length the valley is characterized by steep, sharply defined walls on both its eastern and western sides.
- Between the Danakil Depression in northern Ethiopia and Lake Tanganyika there are at least 30 active or semi-active volcanoes.

Below: *The dazzling snows of Kilimanjaro, only 3° south of the equator.*

THE LAND

Tanzania measures 945,087 km² (364,898 sq miles) in area and contains the highest mountain in Africa, Kilimanjaro (5896m; 19,340ft), and part of its deepest lake, Tanganyika (358m; 1174ft). But statistics alone can convey nothing of the variety or attractiveness of Tanzania's topography, which ranges from mighty volcanic and ancient crystalline mountains to rolling table-land, from great lakes to seemingly endless grasslands, dense miombo woodland to palm-fringed coral sands.

The land is riven north to south by the eastern arm of the **Great Rift Valley**, the western fork of which, in the shape of Lake Tanganyika, helps to form Tanzania's western border. The country's eastern border is determined by the Indian Ocean, and in the south by the Ruvuma River. To the north the border with Kenya is more political than natural, except for a distinct kink around Kilimanjaro.

Mountains and Valleys

The best-known mountain in all Africa is surely **Kilimanjaro**, affectionately known as 'Kili'. Its familiar snow-capped dome rises regally from the Maasai plains in the north of the country. Close by is **Meru**, another beautiful volcanic mountain, and further west other orphans of violence proliferate in and around the Rift. Among them is Ol Doinyo Lengai, 'the Mountain of God' to the Maasai, and still active.

Around Lengai the Rift is dramatic, with abrupt walls to east and west rising to between 270 and 680m (800 to 2000ft) above the floor. The sector of the Tanzanian Rift which most tourists cross, between Makuyuni and Lake Manyara, is less impressive as the eastern wall has eroded, though there are excellent views from the heights of the western escarpment. Beyond the Rift rise the **Crater Highlands**, including Ngorongoro, the most famous crater (more properly caldera) on Earth, and home to as many as 20,000 big game animals.

South of Kilimanjaro, the broken ranges of the **Eastern Arc** mountains ride south in craggy splendour. The light and cloud effects along these mountains, the **Pare** and the **Usambara**, can be spectacular. Further south the ranges swing inland to become the **Ulugurus** and **Udzungwas**, before merging into the **Southern Highlands**, a beautiful region centred around the small towns of Iringa and Mbeya. Southeast of Mbeya the **Livingstone Mountains**, named after the celebrated explorer, shelve with precipitous grandeur into the waters of Lake Malawi (a body of water still known as Lake Nyasa by many Tanzanians).

Above: *A typical first view of Ngorongoro, from the southern rim of the crater.*

TOURING TANZANIA

Tanzania is a very poor country with a gradually developing tourism sector. Things are improving, but sometimes simple things can take much longer than anticipated, so bear in mind that a tour including Serengeti, Ngorongoro, Kilimanjaro and Zanzibar, for example, will easily fill a fortnight.

Visitors are advised to employ the services of a reputable tour company, arranged before or after arrival in Tanzania. For information on reputable tour companies and what they offer, *see* the Travel Tips section at the back of the book.

Above: *The Rufiji River, life-blood of the mighty Selous Game Reserve.*

MONSTERS OF THE DEEP

Tanzania's inland waters can be huge and violent, as can some of the monsters living in them. Lake Victoria is the size of Scotland and Lake Tanganyika, almost deep enough to engulf five Eiffel Towers standing one on top of each other, is longer than Portugal. Both lakes are subject to fierce and sudden storms with 6m (20ft) swells, but beneath their surface live creatures equally daunting. The Nile Perch can exceed 227kg (500lb) and has been known to attack boats. A lungfish in Lake Victoria grows as long as 2m (7ft) and is capable of removing human fingers. Not surprisingly, stories of African equivalents to the Loch Ness monster are traded in the lakeside fishing communities.

The mountains and the Rift dominate their immediate landscapes, but the characteristic topography of Tanzania is the undulating **central plateau**, which averages 1200m (4000ft) above sea level. This tableland, which extends throughout much of the country, can be divided (roughly from northwest to southeast) according to its vegetation. In the northeast open grasslands and Acacia-commiphora woodland predominates, while in the south miombo woodland (mainly Brachystegia and Julbernadia) covers much of the landscape. The plateau, unvisited by tourists, can be a place of great beauty, especially in the rains.

Inland Waters

Tanzania contains more surface water than any other African country. It is drained by a network of rivers, many of them seasonal, and along its western border lie the great lakes of **Victoria**, **Tanganyika** and **Malawi**. Victoria is the second largest and Tanganyika the second deepest lake in the world. The largest river is the **Rufiji**, which drains a vast 177,400km^2 (68,500 sq miles) of land. Other significant rivers are the **Pangani**, which flows south from Kilimanjaro, the **Wami**, which waters two game areas, Mikumi and Saadani, and the **Ruvuma**, which forms Tanzania's southern border with Mozambique. All empty into the Indian Ocean.

Seas and Shores

Tanzania's 800km (500-mile) coastline is typically tropical, with a coral reef and long stretches of white sand, often backed by groves of coconut palm or stands of feathery casuarina. Here and there this congruity of sea and sand is broken by estuaries or mangrove swamps, and in places low limestone cliffs and sea caves.

Fascinating ruins at **Kilwa** and on **Zanzibar** tell of the coast's history, while **Bagamoyo**, just opposite Zanzibar, became prominent as a mainland terminus of both the slave and ivory trade and the exploration of the interior. It lost its status when the Germans, recognizing the excellent natural harbour at **Dar es Salaam**, moved their administrative headquarters south in 1891. North of Bagamoyo is another interesting stretch of coast, including Saadani National Park, Pangani and Tanga.

Zanzibar lies low on the horizon opposite Bagamoyo, and often in cloud, as if mindful of its somewhat murky past. Nowadays, however, both Zanzibar and **Pemba** (to the north) are engaged in more innocent business, bringing in boatloads of tourists rather than slaves. A similar emphasis also inspires **Mafia Island**, which is further south and known for its big game fishing, snorkelling and diving. A marine park is now established there.

MORE MONSTERS OF THE DEEP

Tanzania's offshore waters offer superb fishing. Kingfish, barracuda, giant trevally and grouper are to be found on the reefs year round. From December to March and in August and September sailfish, wahoo and dorado provide exciting sport, with yellow fin tuna from August to December. And if fishing doesn't appeal, you might bump into humpback whales (hopefully not literally). The whales migrate north in July and August to the east of Zanzibar and Pemba. Around October they return, passing between the islands and the shore. Sperm whales and great white sharks are also found in Tanzanian waters.

Below: *Secluded sands and exposed coral at Matemwe, on Zanzibar's northeast coast.*

SHORT RAINS, LONG RAINS

On the equator, the sun passes its zenith twice a year. Because of the phenomenon known as the intertropical convergence zone, about four weeks later the northeast and southwest trade winds converge, causing torrential rainfall typical of the tropics. Generally speaking, the **Short Rains** (mid-October to mid-December) are lighter and much less predictable than the **Long Rains** (mid-March to mid-May). Even during the long rains there can be dry and sunny days in most areas, though visitors can assume that April, throughout East Africa, will be pretty wet. This is not necessarily a deterrent to travel. Most parks and tourist attractions are quite accessible even in April, and in terms of scenery often are at their best.

Opposite: *Flat-topped acacia give attractive definition to the grasslands of Serengeti National Park.*

Climate

The climate of much of Tanzania is dictated by the two seasonal Indian Ocean trade winds, or monsoons, though across the country there are many local variations, mainly due to altitude differences and by the presence, in the west, of large bodies of surface water.

The northeast trades (*kasikazi* in Kiswahili) blow from late December to the beginning of March, bringing the **Short Rains**, the less welcome heat of the Arabian Gulf, and a sometimes oppressive sultriness to the coastal regions. On its tail, from approximately mid-March to mid-May, come the **Long Rains**, *mwaka*. The southeast trades, which generally blow from May to the end of September, curve in from the southern oceans, bringing pleasantly cooler, less humid air across the coast and far inland. Its arrival marks the beginning of the five- or six-month **dry season**, when plant growth, especially away from the coast, comes to a standstill and many watercourses cease to flow.

Because of the country's varied topography, the climate of Tanzania is not as predictable as tropical climates often are. Rain might fall, or fail to fall, when least expected, and the two distinct rainy seasons, characteristic of equatorial regions, will sometimes merge into one or vary considerably in length and intensity. On the whole, however, visitors to northern Tanzania can expect to find dry weather between June and the end of October, and a shorter dry spell from early January to mid-March. Further south the two rainy spells might not be so distinct, with variable precipitation likely from mid-November through to about mid-March.

Temperatures are also changeable, ranging from an average day-time figure of 30°C (86°F) at the coast, where the humidity is often high, to Arctic

COMPARATIVE CLIMATE CHARTS	NGORONGORO				ZANZIBAR				IRINGA			
	SUM	AUT	WIN	SPR	SUM	AUT	WIN	SPR	SUM	AUT	WIN	SPR
	JAN	APR	JULY	OCT	JAN	APR	JULY	OCT	JAN	APR	JULY	OCT
AVE TEMP. °F	70	66	64	70	81	79	66	79	70	68	66	72
AVE TEMP. °C	21	19	18	21	27	26	19	26	21	20	19	22
SEA TEMP. °F	n/a	n/a	n/a	n/a	79	84	81	77	n/a	n/a	n/a	n/a
SEA TEMP. °C	n/a	n/a	n/a	n/a	26	29	27	25	n/a	n/a	n/a	n/a
HOURS OF SUN	8	6	7	8	8	6	8	8	7	8	10	9
DAYS OF RAINFALL	10	13	2	8	8	12	6	11	13	4	0	5
RAINFALL mm	99	114	9	74	94	232	46	155	128	25	1	63

temperatures at the summit of Kilimanjaro. They vary seasonally as well, and visitors can generally expect cooler weather from mid-May to mid-November, particularly between early evening and mid-morning, though the sun can still be searingly hot at the height of the day. But even at the hottest times, cooling breezes or showers of rain can help to make life more tolerable.

Plant Life

In keeping with the variations in Tanzania's topography and climate, the country's plant life is richly diverse in form and distribution. Along the coast, **coconuts**, **casuarinas** and **mangroves** are common. Small (and sadly diminishing) remnants of coastal forest occur in patches a little way inland from the shoreline.

Further inland the natural tree cover in the southwestern half of the country is **miombo**, which gives way in the north to the open parkland of flat-topped **acacia** and 'apple orchard' **commiphora**, which so many people associate with East Africa. Undulating seas of grass make up large areas of the Serengeti, the Rift Valley and the plains below Kilimanjaro and Meru. These and other mountains are partly clothed in **montane forest**, and Kilimanjaro's altitude produces bands of fascinating and sometimes indigenous species of flora, including the **giant heathers** along the upper fringes of the rainforest, and the **giant lobelias** and **groundsels** of the alpine moorland zone.

Elsewhere in the country, where conditions are suitable, the **baobab** grows in corpulent and sometimes archaic grandeur, in places forming magnificent forests. And along the watercourses **figs**, **tamarinds** and **palms** add a welcome touch of green to the dessicated bush, even at the height of the dry season.

Wild flowers do not always grow in great profusion, but there is a wealth of species, and when the rains come the bush can hum with vitality and colour. Some species are unique,

Opposite: *Lady killers – Serengeti National Park.*

such as the endangered African violets, and Kilimanjaro's *Impatiens kilimanjari*, an endemic red and yellow varietal of 'busy Lizzie'.

Cultivated plants include coffee, tea, cashew nuts, cloves, sugar and sisal, all important to Tanzania's economy. Maize, wheat, millet, sorghum, cassava, and rice are grown for home consumption, together with bananas and mangoes. A wide variety of vegetables and fruits come from the fertile central and northern regions of Kilimanjaro, Lushoto, Morogoro and Iringa.

Wildlife

There are many reasons for coming to Tanzania, but the main attraction is undoubtedly the country's wildlife and the magnificent habitats in which it is found. An astonishing 25% of Tanzania's land area is given over to protected wildlife zones, and 20% of Africa's larger mammals are to be found within the country. A dozen or more of these, often including **lion**, **elephant**, **buffalo**, **hippo**, **giraffe** and several **antelope** or **gazelle** can easily be seen in the briefest trip to most national parks. Safari guides, on popular tours to the northern parks, feel disappointed if they haven't shown their clients at least 30 species of larger mammals, from the **Big Five** down to hyrax and mongooses. The Big Five as the old hunters knew them – lion, leopard, elephant, buffalo and rhino – are found (with the sad exception of rhino) in most of Tanzania's parks and reserves, though leopards can be elusive. **Cheetah** can usually be seen in the Serengeti (they occur elsewhere but not in such numbers) and rhino in Ngorongoro Crater. There are also **reptiles** such as crocodiles, monitor lizards and snakes, although snakes are seldom seen. Keen birders, assuming they visit several parks and are accompanied by a knowledgeable guide, can expect to tick off well over 100 species (more than 1000 bird species are listed for Tanzania).

It should not be forgotten that Tanzania has Serengetis of the sea as well as the land. The Indian Ocean is rich in fascinating marine mammals, fish and reptiles, and Lake Tanganyika is full of endemic creatures. The rare and endangered **dugong**, several **turtles** and a whole host of **whales**, **dolphins**, **sharks** and **tropical fish** are found around and beyond the coral gardens of the coastal reefs. Marine parks are now being set up.

Conservation in Tanzania

Having a goose that lays golden eggs is one thing; taking care of the goose is another. Tanzania has an admirable record for creating wildlife sanctuaries, but its reputation for conserving them, as with so many other poor countries, has not always been so good. The decade following 1977 was particularly disastrous, with rhinos slaughtered almost to extinction and elephant populations devastated. The poachers were responding to demand, with horn and ivory fetching huge prices in Yemen, Taiwan, Hong Kong, India, China and elsewhere. Most of the carved ivory, interestingly, wound up in the west.

Control of poaching was hindered by poor morale and conditions among wardens, rangers and game scouts, lack of money and resources, poor management, widespread corruption, and by the flood of firearms following the war against Idi Amin in the late 1970s. It must be said, however, that many of the National Parks and Game Department personnel not only resisted the temptation to make easy money but

THE MAGNIFICENT SEVEN

Where you can spot them:
● **Lion:** widespread, though decreasing rapidly outside protected areas. *Almost* guaranteed in Serengeti and Ngorongoro, and usually seen in Tarangire, Manyara, Mikumi, Ruaha, Selous and Katavi.
● **Leopard:** widespread but best chances are along Seronera Valley, Serengeti, and Tarangire.
● **Cheetah:** often seen in the southern Serengeti, on the plains around Ngorongoro, and less often in Tarangire, Ruaha, and Selous.
● **Wild Dog:** much endangered, with unpredictable movements. Likeliest places are Mikumi, Selous, and Ruaha.
● **Rhino:** Ngorongoro crater.
● **Elephant:** Serengeti, Ngorongoro, Manyara, Tarangire, Mikumi, Ruaha, Selous and Katavi.
● **Chimpanzee:** Gombe Stream, Mahale Mountains.

Above: *A game drive through the Selous Game Reserve.*

GOING UP IN SMOKE

One of the biggest conservation problems in Tanzania is deforestation, and one of its biggest causes is charcoal burning. Sacks of charcoal can often be seen along roadsides awaiting buyers. Most of it goes to Dar es Salaam or other urban areas, where consumption is high. It is the cheapest form of energy for cooking. The charcoal burners of the bush belong to an ancient line of craftsmen, but their fascinating skills were once practiced in less populous times, causing little lasting destruction. But it takes 10 tonnes of raw wood to produce one tonne of charcoal, and today Tanzania's woodland is disappearing at a rate of up to 400,000ha (1500 sq miles) a year.

did an excellent and often dangerous job in limiting the poaching menace.

Thanks to such people, the involvement of the Tanzanian Army, the pressure of world opinion, the support of wildlife organizations and the law of diminishing returns, serious poaching has been curtailed though not completely eliminated. There is, however, much poaching for bush meat, and in northern Tanzania even giraffes are sometimes poached as their bones are believed, by certain superstitious people, to cure AIDS. Elephant populations are slowly recovering and black rhino are being bred and gradually released in certain places.

There are other concerns. The greatest of these is the expanding population and its need for land and sustenance. Huge areas of land are being deforested, mostly to provide charcoal for cooking or a great deal of money for dealers in tropical hardwoods. Irresponsible and often illegal hunting is taking place in certain areas, often with the connivance of corrupt officials, leaving many animals indiscriminately killed or maimed. Increasing cultivation is reducing the habitat of wild animals outside (and sometimes inside) the strictly protected zones. Mangrove swamps and coral reefs, and the marine life which depends upon them, are also still threatened.

The authorities concerned are aware of these problems and, with the help of outside organizations and individual benefactors, are doing much to solve them. It will take time and money, and Tanzania alone cannot be expected to cope. Those privileged to enjoy Tanzania's wildlife sanctuaries are already helping by paying for their pleasures, a contribution it can only be hoped will be for the good of all concerned.

HISTORY IN BRIEF

East Africa has been called the 'Cradle of Mankind', though this distinction must presently rest with Ethiopia, where hominid remains dating back 4.4 million years have recently been discovered. Nevertheless, Tanzania's Olduvai Gorge, in the Ngorongoro Conservation Unit, has provided us with Nutcracker Man (*Australopithacus boisei*) and Handy Man (*Homo habilis*), both about 1.8 million years old, and, at the time of their discovery, significant landmarks in the study of man's past. In 1978 at Laetoli, just south of Olduvai, Mary Leakey found footprints of three upright-standing hominids in compacted volcanic ash, which had powdered the plains 3.7 million years ago.

More recently the aboriginal inhabitants of present-day Tanzania were hunter-gatherers. Other tribes gradually moved in, seeking better land and displacing or absorbing the aborigines. The newcomers were Bantu, entering from the regions between the western lakes. By AD 1300 they had spread into the areas of heavy rainfall, leaving the plains to the Nilo-Hamitic pastoralists who came down later from the north.

DHOWS

As late as 1946, 678 foreign dhows came into Zanzibar, a total probably unsurpassed in East African history. But the large and beautiful *baghlahs* and *booms* (the word 'dhow' is generic and there are many specific types) have become extinct, or are almost so. *Jahazis* of over 9m (30ft) can still be seen, along with smaller *daus* and *mashuas*, the outrigger *ngalawas* and the dug-out *mtumbwis*. Dhows ply the Zanzibar Channel, carrying anything from cloves or cement to chicken feed or corrugated iron, yet few craft evoke the romance of the eastern seas more strongly, leaning into a marbled blue sea, its lateen sail stretched into graceful curves by a steady monsoon.

Arrival of the Arabs

The first non-Africans to visit the area were probably **traders** from Arabia, Persia and India, who eventually settled along the coast with the aim of taking better advantage of trading opportunities or simply because the fertile, relatively peaceful coastal strip was preferable to conditions at home. Being dependent upon the monsoons they would have been obliged, in any case, to stay in East Africa for months at a time.

This settlement of the 'Land of Zinj' (Land of Blacks) began with **Arab** immigrants in about AD 800, who were joined 400 years later by **Shirazis** (originally from Persia). Intermarriage between these newcomers

Below: *All our yesterdays; relics of early man in Olduvai Gorge museum.*

and local Africans produced the **Swahili** people who soon established a rich and enterprising civilization. The resulting language, Swahili, is now spoken throughout East Africa.

Arab and African lifestyles effectively fused into the common Swahili culture, and by the 15th century 37 Swahili towns existed in Zinj. Despite constant bickering among these tiny 'city states', commerce flourished until 1498, when the arrival of Portuguese navigator **Vasco da Gama**, stopping off from his remarkable passage to India, signalled a new era.

The Portuguese Centuries

Above: *A Swahili girl stands by an ornate Zanzibar door.*
Opposite: *Caves used to hide slaves after the trade was abolished in 1873 at Mangapwani on Zanzibar.*

Da Gama, and the compatriots who followed in his wake two years later, were not interested in colonizing Zinj, and made little effort to explore the interior. The Portuguese who found themselves on the Swahili coast were guardians rather than settlers, maintaining bases from which ships could be provisioned and the safety of the shipping lanes between Portuguese territories in

---

HISTORICAL CALENDAR

3.7 million years BC hominids leave footprints at Laetoli.
750,000 years BC Volcanic Kilimanjaro formed.
AD800 Arab traders settle on East African coast.
AD1000 Bantu tribes moving in from west; on coast Swahili civilization beginning.
1498 Arrival of Vasco da Gama. Portuguese rule coast.
1600 British ships appearing in Indian Ocean.
1699 Omani Arabs seize East coast. Portuguese retreat.
1800 Maasai spreading southwards into northern Tanzania.
1832 Seyyid Said transfers

seat of sultanate from Oman to Zanzibar. Era of prosperity for Zanzibar begins.
1860 John Speke leaves Zanzibar to find the source of the Nile.
1871 Stanley sets out from Zanzibar to find Livingstone.
1873 Livingstone dies. Zanzibar slave market closes.
1890 Anglo-German agreement. Mainland Tanzania becomes German East Africa, Zanzibar a British protectorate.
1914–18 World War I. After fierce campaign in East Africa Britain takes control of what becomes known as Tanganyika.
1961 Tanganyika independent; Zanzibar follows

in 1963.
1964 Revolution in Zanzibar. Sultan flees. Three months later Zanzibar and mainland become United Republic of Tanzania.
1978 Idi Amin's Ugandan army invades western Tanzania. Repelled and defeated.
1985 President Nyerere is succeeded by Ali Hassan Mwinyi.
1995 First multi-party elections Benjamin Mkapa elected president. (Re-elected in 2000.)
1999 Julius Nyerere, 'Father of the Nation', dies.
2005 Jakaya Kikwete elected President.

Muscat, Goa and Mozambique secured.

They were, however, well-armed and ruthless. By 1509 the Swahili towns, already disunited, were subdued, with Kilwa sacked and Mombasa reduced to rubble. For the next two centuries the Portuguese occupied the coast, but they were always insecure, threatened by Turkish pirates and later, at the beginning of the 17th century, by the appearance of an increasing number of British ships.

By 1729, with their Indian empire in disarray, the Portuguese were forced to flee by the **Omani Arabs**. The Omanis had raided Mombasa in 1660, and after the stronghold at Fort Jesus fell, the Portuguese sailed south to Mozambique, leaving little behind but bad feeling, rusting cannon, and a host of introduced crops, such as cassava, pineapples, pawpaws and groundnuts.

The Rule of Zanzibar

The Omani sultan, distracted by feuding and rivalries at home, had to leave his newly won East African possessions to various representatives. The Mazrui family, which had been given authority for Mombasa, took advantage of a change of leadership in Oman and declared an independent sheikdom, attacking other settlements. In response to pleas for help, the new sultan in Oman, **Seyyid Said**, sailed south, capturing Pemba in 1822. He was thwarted in his attempts to win back Mombasa, but he fell in love with Zanzibar, and in 1832 transferred the seat of his Imamate to the island. Said was the power behind Zanzibar's rise, establishing the clove industry that was to prove so profitable, and he was to hold considerable influence over events both along the coastal strip and deep into the interior. He also boosted the turnover of that more sordid business, the trade in human lives.

Slaving had gone on for at least 2000 years, but under the Zanzibar sultans it reached its awful peak. Up to 30,000 slaves a year were brought to Zanzibar in the early 1870s, to work the clove plantations or to be sold in the market. Great caravans left Bagamoyo for the interior, returning with slaves and ivory. Zanzibari traders made fortunes, and helped to depopulate huge areas.

A MOVEABLE FEAST

The Moroccan traveller, **Ibn Batuta**, visited the East African coast in 1331, and remarked that the people he found were 'very fat and corpulent'. Though the Swahilis enjoyed a rich diet, they couldn't compete in terms of protein sufficiency with the Zimba, another coastal people – with a taste for human flesh. When the Portuguese attacked the city states in Zinj, they enlisted the help of these cannibals, who literally ate their way from Kilwa to Malindi. They devoured dogs, lizards and rats, as well as the citizens of Kilwa and Mombasa. At Malindi the Portuguese, perhaps afraid of appearing on their menu, turned on the Zimba, almost wiping them out.

Said succeeded to the Omani throne at the age of 15 by plunging a knife into the stomach of his cousin, the regent, and his first sight of the East African coast was at the head of an invading army. Yet Sultan Said saw himself as a merchant rather than a warrior king. It was his success in dealing with slaves, ivory and cloves that brought prosperity to Zanzibar, and earned him the title 'Said the Great'. A less well-known aspect of his enterprising spirit is that he sold another kind of spirit, brandy, to fellow Muslims. Nevertheless he was a surprisingly simple man, courteous and fair-minded, who in matters of justice was said to treat his own sons and the lowest of slaves as equals.

Below: *A crucifix made from the wood of the tree under which Livingstone's heart was buried in 1857.*

The Great Explorers and the Scramble for Africa

As slaves poured into Zanzibar during the third quarter of the 18th century, a succession of outstanding (if not always likable) men were heading in the opposite direction. It was the age of the **explorers**, when the nagging question of the source of the Nile was eventually 'settled' (by John Speke) and when giants of exploration and/or evangelical zeal – Krapf, Burton, Livingstone, Stanley, Grant, Thomson, Von der Decken and Teleki – strode out on their 'long walks'.

All these explorers passed through Zanzibar, which had continued to prosper under successive sultans, though their power dwindled as the British exerted diplomatic and military authority. Reluctantly, Sultan Barghash closed the slave market in Zanzibar in 1873, and soon afterwards, during the 'Scramble for Africa', the British made various treaties with Germany. They effectively took control in Zanzibar and much of what is now Kenya and Uganda, with most of present-day Tanzania, Rwanda and Burundi becoming **German East Africa**.

German rule was generally regarded as harsh. Its early years were marked by an Arab uprising along the coast, a war with the Hehe, and the Maji-Maji rebellion of 1905, in which the whole southern region united against their German overlords. All revolt was savagely suppressed, but the backlash against the Maji-Maji rebellion left the south devastated and 120,000 Africans dead. In Germany there was much disquiet about such brutality, although the Germans did do more to develop the country than their gentler successors, the British.

Tanganyika and Tanzania

In 1914 **World War I** came to East Africa. German-led forces, under their canny commander Von Lettow-Vorbeck, fell back before the British in a strategic retreat, keeping much-needed British manpower and resources from the Western Front. By the end of 1916, however, the British had established a provisional administration, and from 1922 the country, renamed Tanganyika, was governed by them under a League of Nations mandate.

Left: *Former Sultan's Palace (now a museum) in Stone Town, Zanzibar Island.*

Zanzibar, Pemba and the coastal strip, however, remained in the possession of the Zanzibar sultanate.

By and large the British regarded Tanganyika as a poor relation of their adjacent colony, Kenya. Soon after World War II, the 'winds of change' began to blow and on 9 December 1961 the nation became independent, with **Julius Nyerere** at its head. Zanzibar's independence followed in December 1963 but a month later the last of its sultans was deposed in a bloody revolution. A few months after the revolution an arranged (and still troubled) marriage was convened between Zanzibar and Tanganyika, creating the United Republic of Tanzania.

At the crux of the new republic was socialism, and the radical concept of *ujamaa*, derived from the Chinese Communist system of a village-based economy. Though Nyerere remained popular, his policies were less so, as Tanzania slid into severe economic depression, exacerbated by the break up of the East African Economic Community in 1977, and the war with Idi Amin's Uganda in 1978.

Nyerere stepped down as president in 1985. His successor, **Ali Hassan Mwinyi**, a Zanzibari, took over. In 1995 Tanzania became a multi-party democracy with Benjamin Mkapa as its president. Mkapa was re-elected in 2000 with Abeid Karume becoming president of Zanzibar (re-elected in 2005). President Jakaya Mrisho Kikwete (CCM) succeeded Benjamin Mkapa in December 2005.

THE GREAT EXPLORERS

Tanzania was the hub of many 19th-century explorations into 'Darkest Africa'. Most explorers were remarkable rather than loveable.

- **David Livingstone**, called 'The Good One' by the Africans. A determined man, he often depended upon the hospitality of the slave traders he despised, and Stanley found him not preaching the Bible but instead searching ambitiously for the source of the Nile.
- **H.M. Stanley**, who presumed to meet Livingstone at Ujiji in western Tanzania, and subsequently became one of Africa's greatest explorers in his own right.
- **Richard Burton**, an astonishing personality who was fluent in 29 languages, wrote 43 volumes about his exciting and often dangerous travels, and translated the famous *Arabian Nights*.
- Not to be forgotten are the African and Swahili pioneers. Among them was **Juma bin Rajabu**, who was trading in Unyamwezi in the 1840s when Ludwig Krapf, the first European to explore the interior, was still at a mission near Mombasa. He met Burton and Speke, introducing them to his 18-year-old son, who was to become notorious as the great slaver, **Tippu Tip**.

Above: *Zanzibar State House, designed by British architect John Sinclair.*

Julius Nyerere was educated at a mission school near Lake Victoria, then went on to university in Uganda and Scotland. He became involved in politics on his return to Tanzania, and was at the forefront of movements towards independence. In 1961 he became Prime Minister of the new nation of Tanganyika, establishing his policy of *uja-maa*. Revered as the 'Father of the Nation', and widely known as *Mwalimu*, or teacher, many see him as a sincere but failed idealist. Tanzania's economy collapsed disastrously during his rule, but he did bestow some of his personal dignity upon his country and its people. He was a vocal opponent of repression in South Africa and elsewhere, and under him Tanzania, in a continent ravaged by war and tribalism, remained stable and peaceful. He died, still widely respected, in October 1999.

GOVERNMENT AND ECONOMY

From Independence in December 1961 until October 1995 Tanzania was a single-party state, its government elected by universal suffrage, from the age of 18 years.

In 1977 the original mainland and Zanzibari factions merged to form the Revolutionary Party of Tanzania, Chama Cha Mapinduzi (CCM). The government was dedicated to the socialist ideals outlined in Julius Nyerere's Arusha Declaration (1967), much influenced by Mao Tse-tung's China.

When Nyerere stepped down from office in 1985 his successor, Ali Hassan Mwinyi, helped to bring about a shift from socialist idealism to a more pragmatic, relatively market-orientated style of government. This culminated, in 1995, in a multi-party system under Benjamin Mkapa, who continued the country's economic development, taken up, since 2005, by Jakaya Kikwete.

Economy

Various factors, among them radical socialism, poor management, corruption and the war with Idi Amin's Uganda contributed to Tanzania's economic collapse during the 1970s. Nyerere's well-intentioned policy of 'self-reliance' was seen to be over-ambitious, as his country relied even more extensively on overseas aid.

With Mwinyi's appointment (and among growing internal and external pressures for change) a shift of emphasis occurred, with a gradual liberalization of the economy and the privatization of inefficient parastatals and state-owned companies. Tanzania was still heavily dependent on outside aid but its economy was recovering.

This was continued under Benjamin Mkapa. Mkapa kept Tanzania on course, despite many difficulties (including widespread corruption), earning the support of various international economists and governments. This progress is continuing under President Kikwete (elected in 2005).

Inflation is slowly rising again from a low of about 6% in 2002 but road and electronic communications continue to improve and outside investment, though still deterred by high taxation, corruption and bureaucracy, is cautiously increasing.

The economy still relies heavily upon agriculture, which provides around 85% of exports and employs around 80% of the work force, despite the fact that cultivated crops are limited, due to topographical and climatic conditions, to 4% of Tanzania's land area. Industry is primarily concerned with the processing of agricultural products, together with light consumer goods.

The country remains one of the world's poorest but prospects are brightening. Recent years have seen small improvements in industrial output and significant advances in mining, particularly gold. Natural gas is flowing and there are hopes of finding oil. Tourism, after suffering a few setbacks in the 1990s and early 2000s due to internal and external events, has recovered well and continues to expand. With a 16% (approximately) share of the country's GDP it is an increasingly important contributor to Tanzania's economy. Meanwhile banking reforms have helped to improve private sector growth and Tanzania's GDP figures indicate a happier economic future for one of Africa's most deserving countries.

Natural Resources

Tanzania is not so much one of the world's poorest nations as one of its least developed. It is rich (if one includes its astonishing range of tourist attractions) in natural resources, among which are also gold, diamonds, gemstones (including Tanzanite – classed as a precious stone), nickel, iron, phosphates, hydropower and possibly oil. Cash crops include coffee, tea, cotton, sisal, tobacco, cloves, cashew nuts, pyrethrum and seaweed.

TANZANIA IN NUMBERS

- **Population**: 39 million (expected to double by 2025).
- **Birth rate** per 1000 population: 35.95 (world ave. 27.1).
- **Death rate** per 1000 population: 13.36 (world ave. 9.9).
- **Life expectancy**: male 49.4 years; female 52.0 years.
- **Enrolment at Primary Schools**: 96.1%.
- **Secondary Schools**: 8.4%.
- **Traditional Exports** (US$mn): coffee (83.7), cashew nuts (84.4), tobacco (38.4), cotton (38), tea (32), sisal (5.6).
- **Non-traditional**: minerals (177.4), manufactured products (43.1), petroleum products (0.1). (Figures: 2000 est.)

Below: The fertile, sweeping upland and mountain areas which characterize Tanzania's Southern Highlands.

• Tanzania still has many poor **roads** but most highways used by tourists are now surprisingly good. Many others are being upgraded.

• The **rail** network badly needs upgrading if it is to meet tourist standards. Journeys can be long, uncomfortable and frustrating, but the potential is considerable.

• After a disastrous privatization agreement and part-ownership by South African Airways, **Air Tanzania**, back under State control, is struggling to reassert itself as the national carrier. However, various private companies cover most internal tourist routes.

• **Ferries** operate on the great lakes and across certain rivers, and despite a few tragic accidents are generally reasonable. Ferries between Dar and the Zanzibar Islands run daily and are fast, safe and comfortable.

Below: *A hydrofoil ferry approaches Zanzibar.*

Health and Education

Health care is rudimentary in Tanzania. There are **hospitals** in all major towns and clinics in many villages but most are poorly equipped, though the best Tanzanian doctors have an excellent reputation. Malaria, AIDS, tuberculosis cholera and yellow fever are among the most serious diseases (tourists should not be over-concerned – *see* 'Health Precautions', page 125).

Schools are similarly poor in terms of resources and academic performance. Student teacher ratios are sometimes astonishingly high and teachers themselves poorly paid and often unmotivated. Attendance (among students and teachers alike) can be very erratic. Things are improving slowly and sincere attempts are being made to enhance that improvement but the general situation remains unsatisfactory. It will be some time before the extensive reforms now envisaged begin to bring about significant improvement.

Tourism

Until recently most of Tanzania's wonderful and diverse tourist attractions were poorly promoted but things have changed and tourism has recently overtaken agriculture as the country's main export earner.

Assuming that Tanzania maintains its well-established political and social stability and assuming that the present global slow-down does not become a prolonged recession, the country's tourism industry should continue to expand at a steady rate.

Certainly Tanzania is blessed with remarkable natural and cultural attractions, many of which are still unknown to most outsiders.

Tanzania's policy of high cost, low impact tourism, however well-intentioned, discourages many potential visitors. As new forms of tourism are developed, and established ones extended (eg. through cultural tourism, opening up of little used areas etc.), this policy might be revised without compromising Tanzania's vulnerable heritage.

THE PEOPLE

There are 36 million Tanzanians, from more than 120 ethnic groups. No group is dominant and this, together with the Tanzanians' generally easy-going and tolerant nature and Julius Nyerere's non-factional ideals, has ensured continuing racial harmony.

There are relatively minor racial tensions in Tanzania. Tensions are mainly between 'indigenous' and 'non-indigenous' citizens, 'non-indigenous' usually referring to people of Indian origin, though most 'local Asians' get on quietly with their lives and many work happily alongside 'indigenous' counterparts.

A greater concern, perhaps, is the Muslim/Christian situation. About 80% of Tanzania's population is fairly evenly divided between the two, and strains, exacerbated by political affiliations, sometimes show through.

Most visitors, however, will remain unaware of any underlying unease, and find Tanzanians, of whatever religion or ethnic origin, friendly, peace-loving and very hospitable.

23%	Sukuma	6%	Gogo
18%	Swahili	6%	Ha
7.5%	Nyamwezi	4%	Kuramo
7%	Chagga	3%	Hehe
7%	Haya	1%	Maasai
7%	Makonde	10.5%	Others

THE TRIBAL GROUPS
OF TANZANIA

Ethnic Groups

It should be noted that the **Maasai**, fascinating and photogenic as they are, are not the only people in East Africa, and certainly not in Tanzania. 95% of native Tanzanians are actually of Banto origin, rather than Nilo-Hamitic, and the Maasai are, as we have seen, only one of more than 120 ethnic groups.

Below: *Maasai elders in the Rift Valley.*

Above: *Datoga lady with baby, Lake Eyasi region.*
Opposite: *A village near Lake Rukwa in southwestern Tanzania.*

The Maasai, of course, are undeniably attractive, and traditional pastoralist lifestyles are undoubtedly colourful. And as one of Tanzania's main tourist routes cuts across Maasailand these engaging people are hard to ignore.

But located between the Rift Valley and Ngorongoro is the fertile Mbulu Plateau, which most tourists also cross. It is home to the **Iraqw** (known as 'Mbulu' though they dislike the term). Not so immediately striking as their Maasai neighbours, the Iraqw, of Cushitic descent with fine-featured northern faces, are just as interesting. Unlike the Maasai they are cultivators as well as cattle herders.

An hour-and-a-half's drive south of Ngorongoro, by the northern shores of Lake Eyasi, two most unusual peoples live side by side, in this dry, rocky country through which streams sometimes meander in swathes of rare beauty. The **Datoga** are pastoralists and former enemies of the Maasai. Their 'warriors' are renowned lion killers, their girls sometimes so good looking, especially when dressed in traditional beaded leather, that they would, if they could tread the catwalks of London, Paris or New York, leave the western fashion world gasping.

Alongside them live the **Hadza** hunter-gatherers, perhaps the most interesting of all Tanzania's peoples. They eschew most 'civilized comforts' and do not build huts, preferring rudimentary shelters of natural vegetation, caves or even the bare earth. Sometimes they sleep in trees, like the baboons whose meat they prize more than any other. They use powerful longbows and poisoned arrows to bring down game as large as elephants and buffalo, but for most of the year live on wild berries, tubers, birds' eggs and honey. Naked but for simple shorts or aprons, sandals and a few beads, they might not seem unusual but they are.

Among the predominantly numerous Bantu groups are the **Sukuma**, Tanzania's largest tribe. They live around the southern and southeastern shores of Lake

Victoria, growing crops (including cotton) and keeping cattle. They are known for their expertise in drumming skills and for their snake dancing, which features huge pythons.

Other Bantu groups that tourists might encounter include the **Chagga**, who traditionally inhabit the lower slopes of Kilimanjaro and provide porters for the climb to the summit. But the sharp and enterprising Chagga are also to be found throughout Tanzania, wherever there is business to be done.

Visitors to Dar es Salaam will have the opportunity to meet the **Makonde**, in the handicraft market (the actual Makonde homelands straddle the Tanzania/Mozambique border in the southeast). For the Makonde, expert stilt dancers, are better known for their fine wood sculptures, carved from African blackwood (commonly called ebony).

Travellers to the lovely Usambara Mountains will meet the gentle **Pare**, and around Dodoma on the central plateau the **Gogo**, who once resisted the Maasai. Tourists exploring the magnificent 'southern circuit' will encounter, near Iringa, the **Hehe** who resisted not only the Maasai but also the might of the colonial Germans. All are **Bantu**, of which there are more than a hundred others, just as worthy of mention. The best way to get to know them is to meet them in person, preferably through a locally organized 'cultural tour'.

THE MEN OF MAASAI

Traditional Maasai males:
- At the age of **four** or **five**, have two central lower incisors removed (to allow for feeding in case of lockjaw). They are given responsibility for the family's lambs, kids, and calves.
- At the age of **six**, have their upper ear lobes pierced. Given responsibility for slightly older animals.
- At **puberty**, expected to undergo circumcision without anaesthetic.
- After an interim period, become junior warriors *ilmurran*; live with younger girls and the girls' mothers in a *manyatta* (warrior camp).
- At about **20**, become senior warriors.
- At about **27**, they become junior elders, and are allowed to marry.
- In their **30s**, join ranks of senior elders.
- In **old age**, cared for as *desati*, retired elders.
- On **death**, are put out in bush to be eaten by hyenas etc. Only distinguished elders and *loibons* (Maasai prophets) are buried.

Village Life

The lifestyle of most Tanzanians is hard and limited, especially for women in the villages, who do much of the work as well as bearing and bringing up children. The birth rate is high and life expectancy low, although the latter is gradually improving. Villagers in particular spend much of their lives struggling to make ends meet; producing enough food (often with primitive tools), building huts, gathering fuel and fetching water. Life in the towns is, on the whole, seen as preferable (hence an increasing urban drift), though most people find that life is still a constant struggle to make ends meet.

Religion

Many rural people are animist, but most Tanzanians are Christian or Muslim. The Muslims, mostly living along the coast and in Zanzibar, represent about a third of the population, Christians about 45%. The small Asian communities are mostly made up of Hindus, Sikhs and Muslims.

Sport and Recreation

The sporting passion among men and boys is **soccer** (football). Favourite teams are fervently supported in the large towns, and even in the villages boys will be seen kicking around a ball made of rags. **Boxing** and **wrestling** enjoy a minority following among the men, with **darts** being common in many bars and clubs. **Netball** is popular with women, and **volleyball** is sometimes played by both sexes.

Right: *Bao, a traditional game played with beans and a wooden board with cups scooped out of it, being played on Mafia island.*

Water sports are not as popular with Tanzanians as one might expect in a country with a wonderful coastline and many lakes and rivers. Bilharzia (and sometimes hippos and crocodiles!) are a problem in freshwater lakes, though some people take an occasional dip in the sea.

Most Tanzanians love **music** and **dancing**, Zairean rhythms and bands being especially popular. And they love **conversation** (often sexually segregated, with urban, non-Muslim menfolk chatting in bars or clubs over a few bottles of lager, and in the villages in the shade of some tree, perhaps with a home-made brew). Tanzanians are avid readers of newspapers and listeners to radio broadcasts, and a small but increasing number now enjoy TV, videos and even the Internet.

Above: *Worshippers on Zanzibar gather for a musical celebration at a Tarab festival.*

Food and Drink

The **staple** food throughout Tanzania is *ugali* – a stiff maize or cassava porridge. Beans, *mchicha* (a form of spinach) and bananas are also popular. **Meat** is generally too expensive for most Tanzanians to enjoy often. When affordable it usually comes in the form of *nyama choma* (roast meat), barbecued kebabs of goat meat or beef. Barbecued chicken is also a favourite. A stew of meat and plantains (*nyama na ndizi*) sometimes provides a tasty and nourishing alternative. Breakfast often involves deep fried doughnuts (*mandazi*) with tea (*chai*). The combination is appealing though tea (boiled Indian fashion with milk and sugar) might be too sweet for western tastes.

American/European cuisine is regular fare in hotels, lodges and restaurants, with a growing number of international restaurants in the cities and larger towns. A delicious array of tropical fruit is often presented, especially at breakfasts, in the better hotels.

Continental breakfasts are now common in tourist class hotels, though the British breakfast (minus pork products in some places in respect to Islamic obligations) fights a rearguard action. Lunches and dinners in such hotels, lodges and camps are almost invariably adequate and often excellent.

SEAFOOD

With the Indian Ocean as its eastern border Tanzania is a seafood lover's delight. Lobsters, prawns and calamari are readily available in most reputable hotels along the coast, and fish such as red or blue snapper, rock cod, sole, changu, and kingfish all make excellent eating. Lobster, garlic prawns or prawns *pili pili* (with a hot and spicy sauce), as well as various barbecued dishes are some of the local favourites.

2
Dar es Salaam and the Coast

Dar es Salaam is not particularly old or beautiful, but it is interesting and attractively situated. It has a disarming lack of pretension and its people, on the whole, are similarly casual and engaging, representing a colourful and cosmopolitan community.

Half-encircled by the waters of the **Indian Ocean**, Dar stands, or rather sleepily sprawls, mid-way down Tanzania's coastline. This coastal strip, 800km (500 miles) long, was once part of the medieval land of Zinj and the surprisingly advanced and enterprising Swahili civilization. It later became a fiefdom of the Zanzibari sultans, who sold it (under pressure) to the Germans during the 'Scramble for Africa'. The area is scattered with interesting ruins, such as those at **Kilwa**, formerly a famous and prosperous Swahili settlement. It is also a shoreline of some beauty, with many fine **beaches** and a sea teeming with fascinating marine life and, where the reefs have not been destroyed by 'dynamite fishing', ornamented with natural coral gardens.

Seventy kilometres (45 miles) north of Dar es Salaam is **Bagamoyo**, whose clusters of Swahili-style homes and old buildings recall its 19th-century heyday when huge caravans bringing slaves and ivory from the interior, and explorers heading the other way, would pass through. Beyond Bagamoyo lies Tanzania's latest national park, **Saadani**, where big game can be found alongside the sea, and further north still are the drowsily pleasant little towns of **Pangani** and **Tanga**.

CLIMATE

The coastal climate is generally hot and humid, with an average daytime temperature of 30°C (86°F). The hottest months are from November to February or March, but from June to October the southeast monsoon brings cooler, drier weather. From March to May the Long Rains bring heavy showers, but the rain rarely lasts all day, and may be alleviated by days, or even weeks, of intermittent sunshine.

Opposite: *Living palm and dying dhow; small symbols of a significant past on Bagamoyo beach.*

Dar es Salaam

DON'T MISS

* **Dar's seafront:** drive from the harbour to the Sea Cliff Hotel on Msasani Peninsula.
* **The Slipway Plaza, Msasani:** still a pleasant place for a simple meal and/or sundowner by the sea, though loud music can sometimes be intrusive. Shops, handicraft market, boat trips to nearby islands.
* **Dar's beaches:** north and south but especially some of those to the south.
* **Mwenge Handicraft Market:** where you'll find the famous Makonde carvings.
* **Bagamoyo:** mainland stepping-off point for many famous explorers. Historical buildings, pleasant beach resort though beach not outstanding.
* **Kilwa:** fascinating history and ruins, fairly remote except by plane but more accessible since new road and bridge constructed between in and Dar.

DAR ES SALAAM

The inspiration behind Dar es Salaam was **Sultan Majid**, ruler of Zanzibar, who in 1866 began to build a palace on the mainland. His 'Haven of Peace' (as Dar es Salaam is commonly translated) was to have been his refuge from a troubled reign on the island, but Majid died in 1870 before his dreams could be fulfilled. His palace has gone, and all that remains of Majid's dreams is a fortified building, the Old Boma, on Sokoine Drive, and one other building nearby.

Seven years after Majid's death his 'Darra Salaam', according to one report, 'teemed with snakes, scorpions, centipedes, mosquitoes and other pests'. The **Germans**, seeking a deep-water harbour, shifted their headquarters down from Bagamoyo in 1891, and by 1914 they had built a railway from Dar to Lake Tanganyika, just in time for the British to take it over during World War I. Appropriately, the hostilities hardly disturbed the Haven of Peace, though the Royal Navy did lob a few shells shorewards, dislodging coconuts and damaging the old State House.

Dar es Salaam under German rule was an organized and pretty place. Even now Dar's shoreline is a pleasure to drive along, with its fine harbour and the blue seas and near-white sands which sweep around the northern suburbs. Like the Germans, the **British** erected various civic buildings and amenities, as well as bungalows and houses surrounded by lawns and gardens, though bougainvillea and hibiscus tended to proliferate rather than the honeysuckle and roses of home.

Away from the centre Dar es Salaaam is still a refreshingly 'green' city, but is becoming less so. Buildings are going up everywhere, many of them high-rise, and road traffic has increased considerably in recent years. However, shops are fairly well stocked, and Dar es Salaam is beginning to reflect a more dynamic and forward-looking Tanzania.

City Centre **

Dar es Salaam is an absorbing, laid-back mixture of east and west, old and new, races, tribes, religions and political philosophies; an all-pervading, often endearing miscellany of mankind. The city can be dirty, hot, humid and unsophisticated, but it is rarely boring, and most people who live there hold it in great affection. It is the country's main port and economic, cultural and political centre. No one seems to have told it that Dodoma, in central Tanzania, has been designated to take over as the country's capital.

Left: *Flamboyant trees add a splash of colour to Dar es Salaam's otherwise unexceptional city centre.*

ASKARI MONUMENT

The Askari Monument pays tribute to the native troops who died in the 'Ice Cream War', the East African campaign during World War I, so-called because the British were convinced that their German enemies would 'melt away like ice cream in the sun'. The monument (*askari* means 'soldier') has come to symbolize the sacrifice made by all the native African troops, in conflicts which were not of Africa's making, but World War I alone caused the deaths, directly or indirectly, of 100,000 of them. The inscription on the monument was composed by Rudyard Kipling.

To get to know Dar it is best to walk, at least around the central areas. The main focal point, in the middle of Samora Machel Avenue, is the **Askari Monument**. Southwest of the monument **Samora Machel Avenue** stretches away in an untidy bustle of pedestrians and traffic, the pavements cluttered with kiosks selling all manner of cheap goods and souvenirs. It is changing rapidly, with smart high-rise buildings replacing many older, dilapidated but often interesting lower structures. Luxury goods to be found in Dar's shops are imported, and visitors can usually buy the same things more cheaply back home. Local products are often of poor quality, though hardwood furnishings, blackwoodcarvings and basketry often represent good value. But newcomers to Dar will experience something of the city's easy-paced lifestyle, and something of its multi-cultural charm.

In the opposite direction Samora Machel heads towards the open sea, by-passing the **old botanical gardens** on one side, and the **National Museum** on the other. The gardens are quite pleasant. The National Museum contains, among other important relics, the skull of 'Nutcracker Man' found by the Leakeys at Olduvai. There are also interesting displays of tribal artifacts and World War I memorabilia. The older part of the museum represents British colonial architecture of the period. Just a little beyond the museum is **Karimjee Hall**, named after the Karimjees, one of Tanzania's notable old 'Asian' families, who donated the building to their adoptive country. The Hall is now used when parliament sits in Dar es Salaam (as opposed to Dodoma).

The seaward end of Samora Avenue terminates close to the **old German hospital**. It too is an interesting building, its lawns, baobabs and blossoming trees enlivening the stone solidity of the hospital itself. Its garden frontage offers a pleasant panorama of the sea and nearby shore.

Just to the south is the **State House**, with its own attractive lawns and trees. The official residence of the President, it is now screened by a wall and railings (photography is in any case forbidden). The British rebuilt it in 1922 from the ruins of its German forerunner, which was shelled during World War I. The original building was sensitively re-designed, its white-painted front acknowledging Islamic influences.

Above: *Old German Hospital still graces the seafront on Ocean Road.*
Opposite: *One of Dar es Salaam's best-known landmarks, the Askari Monument.*

Kivukoni **

Beyond State House, where Ocean Road bends around towards Kivukoni Front, there is a fascinating little corner of Dar. Here the visitor can explore the new **fish market**, watch the ships and small dhows coming and going through the narrow **harbour** entrance, and at the same time observe a captivating spectrum of Dar es Salaam's population going about its business.

Beyond the fish market and the crowded corner by the ferry, the road, now Kivukoni Front, follows the curve of the harbour and offers fine views across the waterway on one side and the old German administration buildings, still in use, on the other. The road, lined by Indian almonds (*kungu*) on its seaward side, eventually passes the old **Dar es Salaam Club** and the **Lutheran Church**, with its cascade of red-tiled roofs, before merging with Sokoine Drive. Nearby is the Toyota Building (once a private colonial home in German times), followed by the old German **Post Office**, **St Joseph's Cathedral**, the recently

SHOPPING IN DAR
In terms of variety and quality, Arusha is a better place than Dar for handicrafts and souvenirs. But among the better products available are: ● Makonde carvings; ● hand-woven basketwork; ● batiks, and the *kitenge* that are worn by most Tanzanian women; ● Maasai beadwork; ● Zanzibar chests – although they are expensive and shipping home would have to be arranged – and other Zanzibar antiques, such as silver necklaces and broaches; ● African music cassettes and CDs sold in most markets.

Right: *The rising edifice of St Joseph's Cathedral.*

renovated **Boma**, **city hall** and the original **railway station**, built in Bavarian style.

Asian District ★

The area enclosed in the irregular square formed by Samora Machel Avenue and UWT Street, and Uhuru and Maktaba, roughly corresponds to the town's central Asian quarter. Here the visitor can absorb a distinctly Indian flavour – both in atmosphere and more literally, for there are places selling spicy snacks such as samosas, *bhajias* (chilli bites), or those eastern mysteries known as *paan*, normally chewed as a digestive after meals. The Asian communities have brought their own colour to the expanding city. Most of them are traders, shopkeepers or business-people, and their peace-loving, family-based cultures, whether Hindu, Muslim or Sikh, continue to contribute to that most attractive of Dar es Salaam's charms, its easy-going cosmopolitanism.

Among these streets it always pays to look up, as well as around. The mosques, temples, little rooms above the shops, and the clutter of tenement blocks almost always have something to offer: an ornate balcony, intricately fret-worked stone screens, an Islamic motif worked into the beauty of a mosque and a thousand and one little glimpses into the day-to-day life among the extended Asian families. Above many doorways you will see a string of dead mango leaves, put up to bring good luck.

Kariakoo ★

Another lively area – even more crowded, and inhabited mostly by Africans – lies to the northwest of UWT Street. It is called Kariakoo. At its centre is a large concrete **market**

hall, but the nearby streets are a fascinating huddle of little *dukas* (shops), selling everything from plastic buckets to clothes, shoes and second-hand car spares.

Kariakoo gives visitors a brief insight into life among Dar es Salaam's more extensive and increasing African population. The majority live in simple Swahili-style huts or in flats in the less salubrious suburbs, but they maintain their own tribal customs and influences. Care must be taken as Kariakoo is off the beaten track for most tourists.

Northern Suburbs **

Hassan Mwinyi Street leads out of town to the north, and along it are three other noteworthy buildings: the *Nyumba ya Sanaa*, or **House of Art**, where visitors can buy a variety of African artifacts such as woven baskets, mats and batiks, the **Greek Orthodox Church** (in Romanesque Basilican style) and the **Ismaili Jama'at Khana**. The latter is a religious community centre for Ismaili Muslims. A little way to the north of Selander bridge by Haile Selassie Road is **St Peter's Roman Catholic Church**, with its perforated screens and barrel-vaulted roof, and the **Little Theatre Club**, which normally has a lively repertoire, advertised in the local media.

Seaward are the green, leafy suburbs of **Oyster Bay**. The bay itself is pretty especially in late afternoon, or under a full moon. Toure Drive, which follows the seafront, continues to Msasani Peninsula. There are three hotels overlooking the sea along this route, the Oyster Bay, the Golden Tulip and the Sea Cliff. The Sea Cliff has an adjoining shopping mall where you will find restaurants and fast-food outlets. There is also a

Below: Nyumba ya Sanaa, *the House of Art, near the Dar es Salaam Mövenpick (Royal Palm) Hotel.*

Above: *Oyster Bay is particularly pretty in the late afternoon.*

branch of the best bookshop chain in Tanzania called 'A Novel Idea'.

At Msasani Bay, on the western side of the peninsula, is the Dar es Salaam Yacht Club and the popular Slipway Plaza with restaurants and another branch of A Novel Idea bookshop. Both Seacliff and Slipway have well stocked European-style supermarkets.

Skirting the Msasani Peninsula to the west, the Bagamoyo Road carries on north passing the **Village Museum**, an authentic collection of traditional style huts, and the **University**, set on a low hill. Close to the university is **Mwenge Handicraft Market**, where the famous Makonde ebony carvers work and display their traditional sculptures. About 24km (15 miles) north of Dar es Salaam is **Kunduchi**, the main beach resort on this part of the coast, and the site of some Arab ruins.

BAGAMOYO

Bagamoyo is now easily accessible from Dar, though the road can be congested in its southern sector. The small town, 70km (45 miles) from Dar, gives the impression of having slept through the 20th century. Its name is said to mean 'Here I lay down my heart', but whether this was a cry of despair from the countless slaves who were brought here, or a cry of relief from the returning caravan leaders and porters, is not certain.

History

As a terminal point on the coast for Arab trading caravans, Bagamoyo naturally became a holding depot for **slaves** brought from the interior. Most slaves were shipped to Zanzibar crammed into dhows. About half of them were kept in Zanzibar to work on the clove planta-

---

KUNDUCHI RUINS

Just inland from Kunduchi Village and adjacent to it are some early Arab tombs among the baobabs and coastal scrub. They are fine examples of their type, with unique pillars inscribed with Islamic chronologies and porcelain bowls set in the pillars. The delicate pottery bespeaks a fine life style among the coastal Arabs of the period, and with bowls from China and England, indicates the extent of the coast's worldwide trade links.

tions and elsewhere. The rest were dispersed, under terrible conditions, to Arabia, Persia and Southeast Asia.

Famous explorers also passed through Bagamoyo. Among them were the brilliant **Burton** and the more taciturn **Speke**, who was soon, during his second expedition with Grant, to settle the age-old question of the Nile. In 1871 **H.M. Stanley**, with 192 men and six tonnes of equipment, strode off at his usual headlong pace to look for David Livingstone. He returned the following year in triumph, though at 31 his hair had turned grey and he was 'fearfully worn'.

Stanley last stayed in Bagamoyo for one eventful night in 1889, when his party (reduced to 196 from an original 708) marched into town after a three-year expedition across the continent. With him was **Emin Pasha**, governor of Equatoria, whom Stanley had rescued from the 'mad Mullah's' hordes. The Germans threw a lavish party at their headquarters (which still exists) to celebrate the return of the explorers. Emin, short-sighted and perhaps made unsteady by champagne, was later found unconscious, with blood dribbling from his ears. 'The Pasha', in the words of Evelyn Waugh, 'had taken a header off the balcony'.

LIVINGSTONE'S RETURN

David Livingstone died as he knelt in prayer in a village hut in what is now eastern Zambia. His faithful Zanzibari servants Abdulla Susi and James Chuma cut out his heart, buried it under a tree, and then took nine months to help carry his sun-dried remains, enwrapped in bark, to the coast. On arrival in Bagamoyo, the men laid down their burden outside the Mission Church, where they announced: 'Mwili wa Daudi' – 'The body of David'. The tale of that journey from the interior is one of the most moving stories in the annals of African exploration. By one of those ironies that seem inevitable in Africa, the body, in a new coffin of zinc and wood, was transported from Bagamoyo to Zanzibar on board *HMS Vulture*, before it was taken to London and buried in Westminster Abbey. The dour Scots missionary, not without humour, would have appreciated the joke.

Left: *The unpretentious streets of a once-important terminus of the slave and ivory trade, Bagamoyo.*

EMIN PASHA

Born Eduard Schnitzer to Jewish parents in Prussian Silesia, Emin joined the Turkish army, and was later appointed governor of the Egyptian province of Equatoria (roughly modern Sudan). When the Arabs turned on him, he was rescued by Stanley, and during the celebrations for their safe return to Bagamoyo in 1889 the Pasha, of poor sight and a little tipsy, fell from a window of the German headquarters. He recovered from his fractured skull but less than two years later, sitting at a table in his tent in the Congo peering at his beloved specimens of animals and plants, Arab slave traders strolled in and unceremoniously cut his throat.

Around Town

Bagamoyo itself is a nondescript collection of *dukas* (small shops) and huts, with a few larger buildings here and there. Some of the shops and houses have elaborately carved doors. Places worthy of note include the old **caravanserai,** the Sewa Haji School, the former **German headquarters** (there are two), and Bagamoyo's oldest building, a fortified **Arab house** begun in 1860. Used at one time as a pen for slaves awaiting shipment, it became a military garrison in German times and a prison under the British. The **Bagamoyo College of Arts**, just to the south of the town, is also worth visiting. A string of pleasant beach resorts lines the beach just to the north of town.

Mission ★★

Close to these beach resorts stands the first Catholic Mission in East Africa, built in 1868 by the Fathers of the Holy Ghost. Originally intended to house children rescued from slavery, it expanded to become a church, a school, and a collection of workshops and farming projects. It was to this mission that Livingstone's body was brought in 1874.

The Mission remains much as it was then. The old buildings and a museum are the main attractions, but visitors might be interested to know that many exotic plants

Opposite: *Swahili ruins at Kaole, near Bagamoyo.*
Right: *The Fathers' House at Bagamoyo's historic Catholic Mission.*

which now grace the streets and gardens of Tanzanian cities were first introduced here. Coffee was also planted.

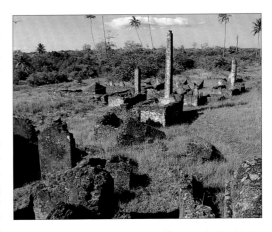

The Kaole Ruins ★★

Five kilometres (3 miles) south of Bagamoyo are the Kaole ruins. They are basically medieval, though some structures (including the West Mosque, once perhaps the finest on the mainland) date back to the 3rd and 4th centuries. Kaole was once the main coastal trading centre between Kilwa and Mombasa, though like other towns of Zinj it declined with the coming of the Portuguese. Among its other notable buildings are a 15th-century house and some double 'love graves', which speak of the prosperous life (and death) styles that merchants enjoyed at the height of the Swahili civilization.

Saadani National Park ★

Recently gazetted as Tanzania's 13th national park, Saadani is also the only East African game sanctuary bordered by the sea. Now almost 1000km² (386 sq miles) in area it embraces a wide variety of habitats, which support an eclectic collection of animal and bird species, including at least 24 large mammals. Among these is the rare Roosevelt sable antelope. Green turtles breed on one of the beaches (Madete) and whales pass through the adjacent Zanzibar Channel in October and November. In the dry season, away from the Wami River, water is scarce and animals less numerous, but the reserve is always worth visiting, except during heavy rains. In Saadani Village, 50km (30 miles) north of Bagamoyo, there is an old German fort and some German graves. Saadoni Safari Lodge, close to the village, organizes game drives and boat trips up the Wami River.

THE BAGAMOYO CATHOLIC MISSION

In 1914 the peace of Bagamoyo was disturbed when the British mounted a naval bombardment and air attack on the town. As the Mission was left unmolested, the Germans moved most of their troops into its grounds, among the mango trees which still line the avenue from the Mission to the shore. Rather touchingly, they took three ancient, ornamental cannons from the Mission gardens and placed them among their more realistic defence battery. The British were neither fooled by the cannon nor deterred by the Mission's neutrality. They pounded the seafront and the mango trees, damaging the Fathers' House and the new church. Miraculously 2000 civilians sheltering in the Mission were unhurt. The German positions were soon overrun by a landing party and the garrison was taken.

Above: *Relics of once prosperous life styles, at Tongoni, by Tanga.*

BEES IN THEIR BONNETS

Sleepy little Tanga was the site of a fierce battle in 1914, when the British landed an 8000-strong assault force, mostly Indian troops, in an attempt to capture the Tanga railway line. Unfortunately the canny German commander, Von Lettow-Vorbeck, was given time to muster his forces. As the queasy assault force hit the beaches and struggled through the bush towards the town with bullets whipping around their turbans, they were attacked by a swarm of bees. It was more than enough for the attackers, who made a hasty retreat, leaving much of their equipment and morale behind. Some divisions took more casualties from the bees than the bullets, although the bullets proved more deadly, killing 800 and wounding 500.

TANGA AND PANGANI

Tanga port stands some 230km (140 miles) north of Dar. Its main street, along which troops of vervet monkeys sometimes roam, has an air of dilapidated colonial provincialism, but the town is a relaxing stopping-off point between Dar and Mombasa, and for dhows crossing from the harbour to Pemba Island.

For a brief time capital of German East Africa, **Tanga** remains one of the larger towns in the country, though with the decline in the sisal industry its economy is in urgent need of revival. There are various places of interest, including the **Amboni Caves**, with limestone formations and colonies of fruit bats, the **Galanos Sulphur Springs** and the **Tongoni Ruins**, as well as some pleasant beaches. It is also possible to drive into the Usambara Mountains from the village of Muheza to **Amani** Nature Reserve, a most attractive area rich in endemic birds and plants.

Pangani, on the estuary of the river of the same name and 45km (28 miles) south of Tanga, offers similarly quiet charms. It had fewer charms for the Arab rebel Abushiri, one of the leaders of an anti-German revolt, who was hanged here in 1897, but present-day visitors might enjoy the waterfront and there are a few interesting buildings, including an Arab fort and some old slave-traders' mansions. There are some very attractive little beach resorts close to Pangani, well worth a short detour for anyone passing through the area.

SOUTH OF DAR

Immediately to the south of Dar es Salaam, across the Kivukoni ferry, are some beautiful beaches and some pleasant resorts, among which are Ras Kutani and Amani. Beyond the beaches immediately south of Dar es Salaam, the coast is still largely undeveloped, its shoreline broken only by the watery maze where the Rufiji slides into the sea.

Kilwa *

One hundred kilometres (60 miles) south of the Rufiji Delta is the once-important settlement of Kilwa. Or rather the three Kilwas – Kilwa Kivinje and Kilwa Masoko, on their mainland peninsula, and the small island settlement of Kilwa Kisiwani. It is difficult nowadays to believe that the Kilwas thrived on gold, slaves and ivory from the the 12th century, when it was first settled by Gulf Arabs, until the 1860s, when something like 20,000 slaves a year were shipped to servitude from its mangrove swamps. As early as 1502, when Vasco da Gama sailed in, an estimated 12,000 'black Moors' were living there.

Kilwa Kivinje retains features of its old Arabic and colonial German associations, and **Kilwa Masoko** still flourishes, though the market from which it gets its name has nothing to do with slaves. But it is mostly the island of **Kilwa Kisiwani** which tourists and travellers seek out, for the ruins there represent the most exceptional examples of early Islamic architecture in sub-Saharan Africa.

The Far South

The rest of the Tanzanian coast, south of the Kilwas, awaits discovery and development. **Lindi** and **Mtwara**, located in the far south, are drowsily starting to awaken to the potentials of tourism, which are substantial. Apart from some fine beaches the area has much to offer in terms of diving and fishing (and perhaps in the future whale-, dolphin-, dugong- and turtle-watching). A promising game reserve (Luwika-Lumesule) lies within striking distance of Mtwara.

THE KILWA RUINS

Here are some highlights of the outstanding ruins on Kisiwani Kilwa:

• The magnificent **Great Mosque**, beautiful even in decay. Built in the 12th century, it was partly reconstructed in the 15th.

• Close by is the **Small Domed Mosque**. This, with its dome surmounted by a unique octagonal tower and its vaults once adorned by porcelain bowls, is perhaps the best-preserved of the island's ruins.

• One of the most impressive of the old buildings is **Husina Kubwa**, which commands a fine view across the straits from its vantage point on a projecting cliff. Husina means 'fort' in Arabic, but the building is thought to have been the palace of a wealthy ruler.

• There is a fort on the island, the **Gereza**, which dominates the northern shores. It was built by Omani Arabs in the early 19th century, on the foundations of a Portuguese stronghold.

Dar es Salaam and the Coast at a Glance

The coast is best from mid-May to mid-October. Jan–Mar can be uncomfortably hot and humid, but monsoon breezes often temper the air. Rain in Mar–Apr, and to a lesser extent Nov–Dec, can sometimes be heavy and frustrating.

International airlines now fly directly to and from the Julius Nyerere airport, Dar es Salaam (tel: 284 4113/284 4111) and Kilimanjaro airport, Moshi/Arusha (tel: 027 275 4771).

Air Tanzania, the national carrier, is presently regrouping after an unsuccessful merger, but many domestic/charter companies now operate. They include **Coastal Aviation** (tel: 255 (0)22 284 3293), Precision Air (0)22 213 0800 and Zanair (Zanzibar, tel: 024 223 3670). **Long-distance buses** run between most major towns and cities. Scandinavia Express (tel: (0)22 218 4833) is among the best. **Railway** line, TAZARA, tel: 255 (0)22 286 0340, links Dar with Zambia. Rail travel is not recommended. **Ferries** ply between Dar and Zanzibar Town, taking 1½ hours or less. For information, tel: 255 (0)22 2137049. **Travel/safari companies** operate in all urban areas. **Car hire** isn't cheap but services are improving. **Taxis** are cheap but haggling is advised and fees should be agreed before setting off.

Dar es Salaam

Mövenpick Royal Palm, tel: (DSM) 211 2416, dirsales@cats-net.com www.royalpalmdar.com Close to town centre and golf course. Upper-end hotel.
Sea Cliff, tel: (0)22 260 0380. Upper end of range in fine location by Indian Ocean, at head of Msasani Peninsula.
Holiday Inn, tel: (0)22 213 7575. Mid-upper range hotel just east of city centre.
New Africa, tel: (0)22 211 7050. Upper end of range, city centre.
Kempinski Kilimanjaro Hotel, tel: (DSM) 213 1111, sales. Kilimanjaro@kempinski.com Upper-end hotel, city centre.

Beach Hotels Close to Dar

NORTHERN
Bahari Beach, Kunduchi Beach, tel: (DSM) 265 0352, 265 0475/6/7, bbhbuz@intafrica.com
White Sands, Jangwani Beach, tel: (DSM) 264 7620, whitesandshotel@raha.com www.hotelwhitesands.com
Jangwani Seabreeze Lodge, Jangwani Beach, tel: (DSM) 264 7215, info@jangwani.com www.jangwani.com
Belinda Ocean, Jangwani Beach, tel: (DSM) 264 7551, belinda@africaonline.co.tz

SOUTHERN
Protea Hotel Amani Beach, mobile: 0741 410 0033, 0741 351257, abc@twiga.com www.proteahotels.com

Ras Kutani, tel: (0)22 213 4802, info@selous.com www.selous.com

Bagamoyo Beach Resorts

NORTHERN
Traveller's Lodge, tel: (Bag) (0)23 244 0077. Probably the best of the various northern extension resorts.
Paradise Resort, cell: 0754 000 904/5, tel: (0)23 244 0136. One of the better of the various northern extension resorts.

SOUTHERN
Lazy Lagoon, cell: 0811 327 706. Desert island-type resort in Lazy Lagoon, little way south of Bagamoyo Town.

Saadani

Saadani Safari Lodge, tel: (DSM) 277 3294 mobile: 0811 323318, www.saadani.com
Tent with a View, tel: (0)22 211 0507/215 1106. Tented camp by the sea.

Tanga and Pangani

The Tides Lodge, mobile: 0741 325812, info@the tideslodge.com www.the tideslodge.com Award-winning resort south of Pangani.
Eyamani Beach Lodge, south of Tanga, tel: (Tanga) (0)27 250 1741, emayani@ habari.co.tz Beach location just south of Pangani.

Kilwa

Kilwa Ruins Lodge, tel: +27 82 978 4044, cell: (0)748 859 235. On beach just outside

Dar es Salaam and the Coast at a Glance

Kilwa Masoko. Specializes in deep sea fishing.
Kilwa Seaview Resort, tel: (0)22 265 0250/1, cell: (0) 748 613 335. On beach facing Kilwa Kisiwani Island.

Mtwara
The Old Boma, tel: (Mtwara) (0)23 333975/333885, cell: 0754 455 978, oldboma@mikindani.com Overlooking Mikindani Bay, close to Mtwara.

All higher-end hotels have good or very good restaurants. Among the best are those at the **Kempinski Kilimanjaro** and the **Mövenpick Royal Palm**. Specialist restaurants include: **Sea Cliff Village**, head of Msasani Peninsula. This has an open-air food court with adjacent fast-food outlets/restaurants, etc. offering meals of various types.
The **Slipway** complex, Msasani, has four restaurants.
The **Shoppers' Plaza** supermarket complex at Mikocheni offers **Fairy Delights** (simple but good-value Indian-style buffet), **Subway** (sandwich bar) and (upstairs) a very pleasant and comfortable coffee and wine bar, **'The Art of Coffee'**. Independently situated restaurants, listed by main cuisine, include:
African/Continental: **Trinity**, Oyster Bay.
Chinese: **Hong Kong**, city centre, **Schezwan**, northern edge of city.

English/Continental: **George and Dragon pub**, Masaki, **Calabash Café**, Sea Cliff Court (not Sea Cliff Village) Masaki.
Ethiopian: **Addis in Dar**, Regent Estate, Mikocheni.
Indian: **Anghiti**, northern suburbs.
Irish/Continental: **O'Willies Irish Tavern**, Msasani.
Italian: **La Trattoria**, off Kimweri Road, Masaki.
Japanese: **Osaka**, Oyster Bay.
Lebanese (fast food): **Albasha**, city centre and Mayfair Plaza, Mikocheni.
Mediterranean: **Mediterraneo**, Kawe Beach.
Pakistani: **Bali's**, edge of city in Upanga (very good barbecue but no alcohol.)
Thai: **Sweet n' Easy**, Oyster Bay, **Thai Village**, Masaki.

Tours of Dar: A few travel companies arrange these, but don't expect too much.
Excursions to Zanzibar and other Islands: Zanzibar Town is within 1½ hours by ferry so return day trips are quite feasible, though it is better to stay for a few days. Mafia and Kilwa can be reached by scheduled flights.
Safaris from Dar: Various Dar-

based safari companies organize short trips to Mikumi, Saadani or the Selous big game sanctuaries or longer safaris further afield.
Bagamoyo: Bagamoyo is now only one-and-a-half's hour's drive north of Dar, so day trips are easily achieved, though try to spend at least one night in one of Bagamoyo's beach resorts.
Bird walks around Dar: See current copy of *Advertising Dar* (available from various supermarkets, bookshops, etc.) for latest details.
Water Parks: Kunduchi 'Wet and Wild' and **'Water World'**, both a 30/40 minute drive or so north of Dar. Water-orientated entertainments for children (or the young at heart).

Code for Dar: (0)22
Code for Tanga: (0)27
Code for Lindi/Mtwara: (0)23
Police: (mobile) 0741 322999
Dar es Salaam International Airport Information Desk: (0)22 (Dar) 284 4113/284 4111.
Aga Khan Hospital: (0)22 (Dar) 260 1484 (Emergencies, cell: 0784 911 111).
Regency Hospital, Upanga, tel: (0)22 (Dar) 215 3063.

DAR ES SALAAM	J	F	M	A	M	J	J	A	S	O	N	D
AVERAGE TEMP. °F	81	81	81	79	75	75	75	75	75	77	79	81
AVERAGE TEMP. °C	27	27	27	26	26	26	26	26	26	25	26	27
RAINFALL in	2	3	4	11	9	1	1	1	1	2	3	3
RAINFALL mm	49	75	114	289	216	25	27	24	37	63	73	83
DAYS OF RAINFALL	3	5	9	18	13	4	4	5	6	6	6	9

3
The Land of Kilimanjaro

'As wide as all the world, great, high and unbelievably white in the sun. . . .' For a writer who made the adjective an endangered species, four in one sentence is a rare extravagance. Hemingway, we can safely assume, was impressed by Kilimanjaro.

With good reason, for the mountain he describes is remarkably beautiful. And the land over which it rises, in such imposing isolation, is scarcely less so. To the west, beyond farms and fields of coffee, the dark pyramid of **Mount Meru** towers above **Arusha National Park**. Beyond Meru a volcanic landscape sweeps up to the Kenyan border and down towards the **Rift Valley**.

South of the two great mountains stretches the so-called Maasai Steppe, with **Tarangire National Park** in its northwest corner, while southeast of Kilimanjaro the **Pare Mountains** diminish towards the coast in a pleasing swirl of hills, valleys, and eventually savanna, much of it enclosed in one of Tanzania's loveliest game sanctuaries, **Mkomazi**. The Pare ranges are continued south by the **Usambaras**, rich in endemics and scenic splendour.

The two towns found in the region are small, but both are of significance to most visitors. **Moshi**, the quiet, strangely pious centre of the Chagga homelands, stands closest to Kilimanjaro on the mountain's lower southern slopes. Its more secular counterpart and tourist capital of the region, **Arusha**, lies below Meru. Little more than a crossroads on the highway to the famous northern game parks beyond the Rift, Arusha exudes a frontier-town

CLIMATE

The dry months from June to October are cool, especially in the evenings and early mornings, when the mean temperature drops to 15°C (59°F). Daytime temperatures, even in the dry season, can be quite hot on the plains, but humidity is low compared with the coast. The wettest months are March and April, when some park tracks can be impassable, with a shorter rainy season mid-October to mid-December.

Opposite: *Kibo, Kilimanjaro's (and Africa's) highest peak.*

DON'T MISS

*** Kilimanjaro: to climb, to see, or just to be near.
** Arusha National Park: splendid scenery, and walks to Mt Meru.
** Tarangire National Park: loved by connoisseurs; at its finest in the dry season, large concentrations of game.
* Mkomazi Game Reserve: lovely wild scenery, though game is relatively scarce.
* Western Usambaras: Magnificent mountain scenery, centred on Lushoto; good birding.
* Eastern Usambaras: montane forests, Amani Nature Reserve, endemic birds and plants.

functionality, its unpretentious shops as likely to sell clutch plates as curios. But it retains a lingering prettiness which, when its jacarandas are purple-blue with blossoms, aspires to beauty.

KILIMANJARO ***
History and Background

Many tourists arrive in the north of Tanzania at Kilimanjaro International airport. If they land by daylight they will usually be treated to a spectacular view of a most spectacular mountain, which dominates, physically and figuratively, the entire plains from which it rises. Thought to be dormant rather than dead, Kilimanjaro is young in geological terms, having been created during massive eruptions about 750,000 years ago.

Despite the fact that the area of its base is larger than that of Greater London, and that it is said to be the highest free-standing mountain in the world, Kilimanjaro remained unknown to the west until 11 May 1848. On that day the German missionary **Johannes Rebmann**, armed with his Bible and umbrella, fancied he saw, on the summit of one of the 'mountains of Jagga' (as he called the three clouded peaks of Kilimanjaro), a 'dazzling white cloud'. His guide laconically told him that the cloud was *baridi* – cold. Rebmann realized that what he was looking at was snow.

Opposite: *Kilimanjaro National Park head-quarters, the starting point for ascents up the mountain by the Marangu route. The park is soon to be extended, making it about twice its present size.*

His reports were ridiculed by distinguished geographers back in England. The idea of a snow-topped mountain just south of the equator seemed absurd, but the gentle missionary was of course right. It was over 40 years before another German, **Dr Hans Meyer**, and an alpine guide, **Ludwig Purtscheller**, became the first men to climb the loftiest of the great mountain's three peaks, Kibo, at 5896m (19,340ft) the highest point in Africa

The **Chagga** who live on its slopes have no word for the mountain which is at the centre of their lives, only for its two main peaks, Kibo and Mawenzi. No-one really knows how Kilimanjaro got its popular name, but ironically the word *Kilima* in Kiswahili means hill rather than mountain. Perhaps the diminutive was used out of familiarity, for Kilimanjaro (or 'Kili', to many) seems to inspire affection. The famous 'Christmas pudding' mountain is instantly familiar all over the world, often (ironically) from photographs taken from Amboseli National Park in Kenya. Its popularity is enhanced by the fact that many thousands of visitors reach the summit each year, and Kili can justifiably claim to be the highest mountain in the world accessible to non-expert mountaineers. Truly a mountain of the people.

> ### THE CHAGGA
>
> To the Chagga the importance of Kilimanjaro cannot be over-emphasized. The mountain gives them shelter and its slopes sustenance, but above all it gives them an identity: an old, precise, deep-rooted sense of place. A Bantu-speaking race, visitors will meet them as guides and porters on Kili, and they are considered one of the most enterprising, forward-looking people in Tanzania. One feature of their culture is that their language is rich in place-names. The most ordinary stream will have a name of its own, helping to place it in the mental maps and the 'tribal memory' of the local people, and incidentally reflecting the importance of water to a people who can see, from their mountain home, the dust-storms blowing across the baked red earth of the plains below.

Moshi *

Moshi stands on the lower southern slopes of Kilimanjaro, but it is often bypassed on the way to the start of the climb at Marangu. The town has a wonderfully picturesque setting, but is respectable rather than exciting. The international airport is 34km (21 miles) to the west, and the town is also accessible by rail and road. Arusha, an hour's drive to the west of Moshi, is the nearest sizeable centre, while a further three hours' drive to the north and into Kenya is Nairobi, a well-established tourist centre.

The village of **Marangu**, half an hour's drive east of Moshi, is the starting point for most ascents of the mountain. A number of operators are based here, as well as the area's two oldest hotels, the Kibo and the Marangu. Newer hotels and guest houses are appearing. Marangu is a pleasant village with an alpine feel, and lies 7km (4 miles) from the entrance to the National Park gate, which marks the start of the most popular tourist, route up Kilimanjaro.

Climbing Kilimanjaro ★★

From Marangu, at 1500m (5000ft), the mountain can look overwhelmingly high, but would-be climbers have little to fear except the unpleasant effects of altitude sickness. Tens of thousands of people climb Kili every year, and tens of thousands come safely down again. Most people opt for the standard five-day climb, though some people choose to spend an extra night at the second of the trail's three huts, to help acclimatize.

Day One: The first stage of the climb is through the rain forest, a lovely three- or four-hour trek from the park entrance to the first complex of A-frame huts, named after the famous Chagga chief **Mandara**, at 2700m (8850ft). The forest zone, which girdles the mountain, is the second of

Right: *In the dank, sultry air of the rainforest at the start of the climb, the snow and ice of the summit seems a long way away.*

Left: *Day one of the climb, through the forest zone.*

the five distinctive vegetative zones walkers experience on their ascent. It has a characteristic rainforest atmosphere; a damp, green luxuriance which for some people is claustrophobic. Among the mighty trees, festooned with vines and lichens, Sykes or Colobus monkeys are sometimes seen, as is the brilliant crimson flash of a Hartlaub's turaco. As the path approaches Mandara Hut one encounters the first groves of giant heather.

Day Two: After an overnight stop at Mandara, walkers press on (or more wisely saunter) to the second complex of huts at **Horombo**, at 3720m (12,200ft). Skirting Maundi Crater to the west, the track climbs a fairly steep and sometimes slippery bank of rainforest, soon emerging on to the heathland zone, which in turn becomes upland moors. This is beguiling country of open views and muted moorland colours, where modest but beautiful plants abound. The plants are tougher than they look, and it is easy for the walker to forget that this gentle, rolling country is higher than the peaks of the Pyrenees. *Pole pole* is the order of the day, for the last few kilometres of the five-hour walk to Horombo involves some small but deceptively tiring ravines.

> ### BIBULOUS BARONS AND CAROUSING COUNTS
>
> Climbing Kilimanjaro can seem a bit of a dawdle these days, but getting there first was a bit more daunting.
> - In 1861 the German explorer **Von der Decken** attempted Kilimanjaro but saw off his celebratory magnum of champagne (and his chances of reaching the summit) long before he emerged from the foothills.
> - Sixteen years later Hungarian bon viveur **Count Samuel Teleki** and his companion paid similar respects to a bottle of red wine as they camped in the snow on The Saddle. They got little further.
> - In 1889, **Hans Meyer** and **Ludwig Purtscheller** reached the crater rim after an exhausting climb over the crevasse-ridden ice-cap. Weakened and wearied they staggered back to camp, but the next morning (3 October) they returned, eventually reaching the highest point in Africa. Meyer planted a small German flag, the two men shook hands, raised three cheers for their Kaiser, and called the peak Kaiser Wilhelm Spitze – now Uhuru (Freedom) Point.

Day Three: Just after Horombo climbers pass a stream known ominously as Last Water then some low, striated cliffs known as Zebra Rocks. Ahead is the Saddle, the sway-backed ridge which connects Kilimanjaro's two main peaks, **Kibo** and **Mawenzi**. Beyond Zebra Rocks the track forks. The path to the right is the more direct route to the Saddle, the gradual path to the left the more frequently recommended route. Whatever route is taken, the Saddle is not a welcoming place. The five- or six-hour walk is quite gentle, but the last upcurve to **Kibo Hut**, at 4700m (15,400ft), can turn legs to sandbags and make hearts go into overdrive.

Days Four and Five: Kibo Hut is a dreary place at the best of times, with an atmosphere as congenial as a condemned cell in Siberia. Walkers huddle into sleeping bags, not to sleep but to keep warm. Heads pounding, stomachs churning, they wait to be dragged out, at 01:00 or 02:00, into the icy darkness. Then, with a guide leading the way holding a small lantern, each party files into the night up the steep, zigzag track which leads to **Gillman's Point** on the summit crater rim. The early start allows walkers to reach Gillman's by dawn and to see the spectacular sunrise beyond Mawenzi and, with the scree freezing at night, provides a safer footing. But the third

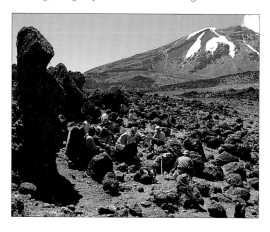

Right: *Kibo peak looms large for climbers on the Mweka route.*

reason for making this final ascent in darkness is to maintain a visual ignorance; if walkers could see what lies ahead, how steep the slope is, how high above them the rocks were that mark the last scramble to the rim, they might well lose heart and turn back.

And so they plod on, mountain sticks tapping out a slow, staccato rhythm. The guide sometimes sings a plaintive song, to placate the mountain, and to take the minds of his charges off their ordeal. At this altitude, oxygen is twice as rare as at sea level; breathing becomes laborious, paced steps and frequent stops are important. Almost every step becomes an effort of will. Halfway to Gillman's Point (and about two hours above Kibo Hut) is an overhang known as Hans Meyer cave, in which walkers often take a breather.

Above the cave the track rises very steeply. Walkers are faced with a further two hours of will and energy-sapping endeavour. At Johannes Notch, on the crater rim, there is a last heavy-legged scramble to Gillman's, and relative relief. Few people leap around in triumph, though the view which is revealed to them, as the sun climbs up beyond the turreted peaks of Mawenzi, far across The Saddle, usually gladdens the thumping heart. Even so, after a brief rest and group photographs, many people opt for those three much-recommended cures for altitude sickness – descent, descent, descent.

Above: *Evening light on the exposed Barafu spur, one of the setting-off points for the final early-morning push to the summit.*

STRANGE THINGS AT THE TOP OF AFRICA

Animals, as well as flowers, have been seen at the top of Kilimanjaro, including the frozen carcass of a leopard, mentioned by Hemingway in *The Snows of Kilimanjaro*, and a small pack of wild dogs reported by that great explorer, Wilfred Thesiger. Odd things have gone on there too. Parachutists have landed on Kibo, hang-gliders have jumped off it, it has been climbed by a pair with their legs tied together, a party of blind people, an 85-year old Spaniard (who vows he'll be back when he's 90), a motor-cyclist has conquered it and a game of tiddlywinks has been played at the summit.

ARRANGEMENTS FOR CLIMBING KILIMANJARO

• Registered **guides** are obligatory, porters very much recommended.
• Most people climb Kilimanjaro via **package deals** through home-country travel agencies. Independent travellers will find operators in Arusha, Moshi or Marangu.
• A trek can cost from $2000–$5000 per person, depending on the company and the route. The fee includes camping, food, guides, park fees and transport to and from the mountain. It is probably best to spend at least $2400 per person.
• Cheaper climbs are available but not necessarily good value.
• Individuals can 'tailor' their own climbs but should allow extra time for this.
• Warm **clothing** and wind-and-waterproof outers are essential (several light layers are better than a cumbersome one). Appropriate footwear, sleeping bag, sun protection and water bottles are among other necessities. Equipment can be hired in Marangu but climbers should not cut corners to save cash.

Kilimanjaro National Park

<2100 m	3900 m - 4500 m
2100 m - 2700 m	4500 m - 5100 m
2700 m - 3300 m	5100 m - 5700 m
3300 m - 3900 m	>5700 m

0   5 km
0   3 miles

But the experience will live with them forever. And the punishment and pain will all be forgotten. For to look down on Africa, from the top of Africa's highest mountain, is breathtaking metaphorically as well as literally. And the peak itself, with its wedding cake-like terraces of ice, and perhaps a fresh layer of snow in and around the symmetry of its remarkable crater, has a stark and sterile beauty of its own.

The true summit, **Uhuru Point**, is 210m (700ft) higher, and a further hour's struggle around the crater rim. For many Gillman's is enough, and almost everyone is glad when the time comes to go down. The descent over loosening scree should be treated with caution, but the long trek back from the base of Kibo to Mandara Hut is covered, by most people, surprisingly quickly (Horombo Hut being bypassed).

Left: *A high camp site on the Shira plateau.*
Opposite: *On the roof of Africa. Smile and pretend you don't have a headache!*

Other Routes

Routes vary in difficulty, popularity and scenic beauty. The least difficult, most popular is **Marangu**, followed by **Rongai**; the more difficult routes are **Machame**, **Shira** and **Lemosho**. The longer routes such as Shira and Lemosho (crossing the Shira Plateau from the west) involve more hiking but better acclimatization. They also allow you to start your summit hike at less 'anti-social' hours!

The **Machame** route (from the southwest) is one of the more beautiful, as it ascends through the forest to emerge on the Shira Plateau, facing the magnificent Western Breach with its daunting Wall, though the route has become much more popular in recent years. The **Umbwe** and **Mweka** routes also pass through the forest, from the south, whilst in the west are the longer but more gradual routes across the Shira Plateau, the **Shira** and the **Lemosho**.

Vegetation

One of the many interesting effects of a five-kilometre-high free-standing mountain on the Equator is that it embraces a complete range of vegetational zones. On the lowest slopes, up to a height of about 1800m (5900ft), the land, of rich volcanic soil, is used for **pasture** and **cultivation**. The next zone is composed of **rainforest**. With an annual rainfall of over 2000mm (79in), it is lush, dense, and often girdled by mist. The rain and condensation

A FEW COMMON BIRDS OF THE MOORLAND

Kilimanjaro's famous giant lobelia hides some pretty flowers, which are visited by scarlet-tufted malachite sunbirds. The male is a metallic green bird with a long tail, its tiny scarlet tufts sometimes visible on either side of its chest. The smaller Eastern double-collared sunbird is also found here. Other, less colourful birds to be seen on the moorland include augur and mountain buzzards, Shelley's francolins, Cape quail, Alpine swifts, stone chats, Hunter's cisticolas and yellow-crowned canaries. Alpine chats, streaky seed-eaters and white-necked ravens might be seen around Horombo Hut. The chats are as tame and as perkily plump as European redbreasts. They might well be called the 'Kilimanjaro Robin' but they are true mountain birds, at home on the upland moors.

filters through the plants, humus, and porous volcanic rock. The water then runs underground along less porous strata of lava to emerge as springs on the lower slopes, where much of it is channelled into the sometimes ancient and ingenious irrigation schemes of the Chagga. Most of the wildlife found on the mountain occurs in the forest, including elephant, buffalo and leopard, but walkers are very unlikely to encounter them. More common are black and white colobus monkey, or the blue-grey Sykes monkey, along with a number of birds.

From about 2800m (9200ft) to 4000m (13,100ft), the landscape becomes open **heath** and **moorland**. This is characterized by hardy heathers, some of which grow up to 9m (30ft) tall, and giant lobelias and senecios. *Lobelia deckenii*, the only giant lobelia found on Kilimanjaro, can sometimes grow up to 3m (10ft) in height. *Senecio kilimanjari* is one of two giant senecios found on the moors. It too is endemic, and grows as high as 5m (16ft). The senecios have thick shaggy stems, often branched, and are topped by great rosettes of leaves, like giant artichokes with open bracts. Like the lobelias they grow beside streams. Behind Horombo Huts, in the damp little valley below Mawenzi, a whole colony of them stand like monsters from another world.

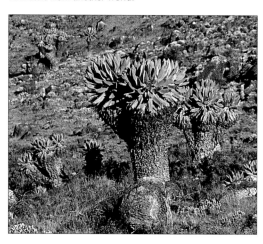

Right: *A rare, giant senecio kilimanjari on the moorland zone.*

Above this, from 4000m (13,100ft), is the **'Alpine'**
desert. It seems very bleak, ranging from freezing temperatures at night to blistering sunlight at midday. This constant
freezing and thawing (called solifluction), loosens the soil,
discouraging the growth of roots, but lichens are common,
while one plant, a moss ball, rolls around feeding on the
soil it picks up and the moisture it absorbs.

Little lives above 5000m (16,400ft), and though the
glaciers of the summit are slowly reducing in size, much
of the ground is constantly under ice and snow. One ever-
lasting flower, *Helichrysum newii*, has learned to live in
Kibo Crater, sustained by the heated soil alongside
a fumarole. It is said to be the highest flower on earth.

ARUSHA

Arusha, 70km (45 miles) to the west of Moshi, is a
livelier town than its neighbour. Situated beneath Mount
Meru, it is base camp for most safaris in Tanzania's
famous northern game reserves. Like many African
towns, it has a half-neglected air, but tourism is bringing
in money, hope and rising standards. A decent range of
hotels, restaurants and curio shops are now springing
up, and Arusha could well develop into the Nairobi of
northern Tanzania.

> **CLIMBING
> MOUNT MERU**
>
> Guided climbs to the 4566m
> (14,990ft) high summit of
> Meru can be arranged through
> the park authorities or various
> safari companies. It is a three-
> day (two up, one down) trip. It
> is a pleasant climb, without
> the crowds or the more severe
> altitude problems associated
> with Kilimanjaro. Costs are
> lower as well, although you
> will need a registered guide,
> and good equipment is neces-
> sary on the upper slopes. The
> most common itinerary is to
> walk from Momela Gate to
> Miriakamba Hut on the first
> day, which allows a chance to
> explore the fantastic crater and
> ash cone. Day two is only a
> three-hour climb to Saddle
> Hut, at 3600m (11,800ft), from
> where the summit (4566m;
> 14,950ft) is four to five hours
> away, and normally attempted
> early the next morning.
> Coming down to Momela
> Gate takes about eight to nine
> hours. The best time to climb
> Meru is between October and
> February. Scenery, at whatever
> time of year, can be splendid.

Left: *Arusha, the unas-
suming hub of Tanzania's
beautiful and fascinating
northern safari circuit.*

Above: *Mount Meru, the 'Black Mountain' to the Maasai, towers above the town of Arusha.*

NGURDOTO CRATER

One of Arusha Park's prime attractions is Ngurdoto Crater. No human incursions on to the crater floor are permitted, and visitors must drive to the crater rim to look down into its entrancing green arena. It is 3km (2 miles) in diameter, and its forests and swamps are home to elephant, buffalo and other creatures. Red duiker might be observed in the forest during the steep ascent, and colobus monkeys, those hand-some acrobats of the high canopy, are often to be seen close to one of the viewpoints on the crater rim.

Mount Meru ★★

Like Kilimanjaro, Mount Meru is volcanic, but its dark peaks and ridges are more mountain-like than the Christmas pudding Kilimanjaro, its collapsed crater floor tucked away amid the forest, far below the summit. This crater is a most impressive place, silent, almost eerie, half-encircled by a ghostly forest of lichen-hung trees. A precipitous ash cone rises from it, backed by its own darkly forbidding wall, over 1500m (4900ft) high. Meru is part of Arusha National Park, and it is possible to walk to the crater through the rainforest, from the park's Momela Gate. The ascent is straightforward and takes about three or four hours (*see* panel on page 55 for details of climb).

There are elephant and buffalo on Meru, and the possibility of strolling around a corner to find several tonnes of muscle and bone twitching, stamping and snorting demands that you are accompanied by an armed ranger. The actual danger is minimal, but there might be times when this is hard to believe. Less threatening creatures live here too, among them the shy and handsome bushbuck. Sensitive walkers, if they stay silent and still, might get good views of these.

Arusha National Park ★★

The park which Meru overlooks is overlooked in a different sense by many tourists, who rush by to more spectacular places, yet Arusha National Park is among the most beautiful in Africa. With Meru in its western corridor, and Kilimanjaro to the east, it encompasses placid alkaline lakes, montane forest and open glades. There are plans for it to be extended so as to include even more. Its rhino have been obliterated and its elephant, harassed by poachers, have largely taken to the hills, but Arusha retains a superb range of flora and fauna. Other mammals in the park include leopard, hyena, baboon, hippo, zebra, giraffe, waterbuck, dik-dik and warthog. Bird life is prolific, especially around the **Momella Lakes**.

THE FRINGES OF THE MAASAI STEPPE
Tarangire National Park ★★

A very different, but even more exciting, national park is Tarangire, across the Ardai Plains west of Arusha. Named after the shallow but important river which passes through it, Tarangire is 'on' when the southern Serengeti is 'off', with huge numbers of game sustained by the river throughout the dry season (roughly from July–October).

Tarangire is one of the few places in Africa where elephants can sometimes be seen in herds of 300 or more, and lion are quite common, especially during the dry season when huge numbers of wildebeest and zebra trek in from the Steppe tired and unwary. Black rhino were once common, but were almost all exterminated in the 1980s. There is also an impressive number and diversity of birds, while the very country itself, particularly in the north areas with their umbrella thorns and elephant-battered boababs, is quintessential 'real Africa'.

Below: *The Tarangire River provides welcome relief in an otherwise dessicated dry-season landscape.*

Right: *Elephants, living barometers of successful management in many game parks, on the move in Mkomazi.*

Mkomazi ★

Across the Maasai Steppe, 125km (78 miles) or so south of Moshi, is another game sanctuary, Mkomazi. Access is via **Same** (rhymes with 'army') township through a gap in the Pare Mountains.

From these lovely ranges German guns once bombarded the British-led forces as they chased their elusive enemies south during World War I. Same is peaceful now, and the Pare people characteristically gentle and obliging. But those one-time warriors, the Maasai, have recently been evicted from the reserve and are fighting (in the courts, not with spears) for what they see as their traditional grazing rights. Any resolution which gives Mkomazi's animals full protection without denying limited grazing to the Maasai would surely benefit the tourist industry. The Maasai are always a cultural attraction, and Mkomazi is a beautiful place, especially after the rains, when its sweeping hills and plains are a vibrant green.

Mkomazi's game is still quite wild despite decades of poaching and hunting, and although visitors might not see as much, in terms of numbers, as they will in the better-known sanctuaries, the reserve is as pretty a piece of bush as you are likely to see in Africa and any animals are a bonus. Possibilities include lion, leopard, cheetah, elephant, buffalo, eland, fringe-eared oryx, hartebeest, zebra, giraffe, Grant's gazelle and the shy aardwolf. The endangered black rhino and wild dog are both being bred, for eventual release in the wild, in the reserve. Birding is excellent.

Lushoto *

South of Same and the Pares are the **Western Usambaras**, another lovely range of mountains. A pleasant 110km (70 miles) drive from Mkomazi, with the mountains to the east and the Maasai plains to the west, brings the traveller to **Mombo**. From here a good road winds up into the Usambaras to Lushoto, 25km (15 miles) away. The drive alone is worth the diversion, for the scenery, especially in good light, is extremely picturesque.

Lushoto, sited on the slopes and terraces of a pleasant upland valley, was obviously popular with the colonial Germans, who, acknowledging its situation and relatively mild climate, thought of making it their capital. Even now the administrative buildings, missions and churches around the town proclaim their European derivation. The vicinity of Lushoto is very fertile, producing vegetables and fruits for the markets of Dar and elsewhere.

WALKING IN THE USAMBARAS

There are some fine walking tracks around Lushoto, many of them gently graded paths leading through the montane forest or up the hillsides. Although widely cultivated, the Western Usambaras offer some magnificent scenery, and the forests protect a spectacular number of endemic plants. One of the most rewarding walks is to a place called The Viewpoint, a comfortable one-hour hike from Lushoto, via Irente. The views from this vantage point, across the course of the Pangani and the Maasai Steppe beyond, are very impressive. Ask at the hotels for other recommendations.

Below: *The expanse of the Maasai Steppe and the small town of Mombo.*

The Land of Kilimanjaro at a Glance

BEST TIMES TO VISIT

The north is generally pleasant all year, though the rains (mid-March to May and mid-October to mid-December) can be inconvenient. The period from mid-May to mid-October is noticeably drier and cooler.

GETTING THERE

A number of **international airlines** fly into Kilimanjaro Airport, between Moshi and Arusha. Travellers entering from Kenya take **chartered flights** from Nairobi or Mombasa or enter by **road**, either with Kenyan-based safari companies or long-distance buses.

GETTING AROUND

Most visitors travel on **pre-arranged package tours**. For independent travellers there are many safari companies in Arusha and Moshi. **Taxis** are available in Moshi and Arusha and there are **car hire** firms in each town, including some of the travel companies. A good **shuttle-bus** service (Riverside) connects Moshi, Arusha and Nairobi (Kenya) twice daily.

WHERE TO STAY

Most tourist-class hotels in Marangu/Moshi area organize Kilimanjaro climbs.

Marangu

(close to Kilimanjaro NP gate)
Marangu Hotel, tel: (Moshi) (0)27 275 6594/6361, marangu@africaonline.co.tz Former farmhouse, in gardens.
Kibo Hotel, tel: (Moshi) (0)27 275 1308. German colonial,

bit dilapidated but plenty of character.

Moshi

AMEG Lodge, tel: (0)27 275 0175/0185. High end, situated among leafy northern suburbs.
Protea Hotel Aishi Machame, tel: (Moshi) (0)27 275 6941, proteaaishi@africaonline.co.tz www.proteahotels.com One of the best hotels in Moshi area. West of Moshi on southwestern slopes of Kilimanjaro.
Lutheran Uhuru Hostel, tel: (Moshi) (0)27 275 4084, uhuru@africaonline.co.tz Simple but excellent value for money, especially 'New Wing'.
Kilimanjaro Crane Hotel, Moshi town, tel: (Moshi) (0)27 275 1114/275 3037, kilicrane@eoltz.com www.geocities.com/The Tropics/cove7585 One of the best hotels in town centre, reasonably priced. Specializes in climbing and game-viewing safaris.
Moshi Impala, tel: (0)27 275 3443/4. Pleasantly located on Lema Rd. in leafy suburbs 2km from town.

Usa River/Arusha National Park Area

(East of Arusha Town)
Serena Mountain Village, tel: (Arusha) (0)27 250 6304, centralreservations@serena. co.tz www.serena.com Quality hotel, beautiful gardens, views.
Dik-Dik (Arusha) (0)27 250 8110, satellite phone: 873 762

06 0473, www.dikdik.ch Small, exclusive, excellent.
Hatari Lodge, tel: (0)27 255 3456. Details as Momella Wildlife Lodge.
Ngurdoto Lodge, tel: (Arusha) (0)27 255 3701/3414/8. Between Usa River and Ngurdoto Gate, Arusha NP. Visited by elephant and other animals.
Ngare Sero Mountain Lodge, tel: (0)27 255 3638, cell: (7) 87 560 055. Old German farmhouse near Usa River, long popular with expats.
Moivaro Coffee Plantation, tel: (Arusha) (0)27 255 3242, moivaro@habari.co.tz www.moivaro.com Excellent little hotel, 20 min. drive east of Arusha.
Rivertrees Guest Farm, tel: (Arusha) (0)27 255 3894, cell: (0) 713 339 873, rivertrees@africaonline.co.tz Small, homely farmhouse situated on Usa River a few kilometres east of Arusha.

Arusha

Arusha Coffee Lodge, tel: (0)27 254 0630/254 8245. Superb lodge 5km west of Arusha Town.
Arusha Hotel, tel: (0)27 250 7777. Bang in centre of town, with pleasant gardens and considerable social history.
Novotel Mount Meru, tel: (Arusha) (0)27 250 2711, mtmeruho@africaonline.co.tz Large hotel, northern Arusha.
Impala, tel: (Arusha) (0)27 250 2962, impala@cybernet.co.tz www.impalahotel.com Immediate outskirts of Arusha.

The Land of Kilimanjaro at a Glance

Tarangire National Park
Inside park:
Tarangire Safari Lodge, (0)27 254 4752, cell: (0) 784 202 777. Best location in park, long-time favourite with old Africa hands.
Tarangire Sopa, tel: (Arusha) (0)27 255 0630-9/0601/6703, info@sopalodges.com www.sopalodges.com Good location in centre of park.
Nomad Tarangire, no direct bookings, but Nomad's (the owning group) tel: (0)27 255 3819, cell: (0)784 734 490. Exclusive, 'Bedouin-inspired' camp in southern Tarangire.
Oliver's Camp, tel: (Arusha) (0)27 250 4116/8548, Olivers@habari.co.tz Amid bush on migration route in east-central park area. Knowledgeable management.
Swala Lodge, remote corner of Tarangire. Luxury tented camp.
Outside park:
Tamarind Camp, tel: (Arusha) (0)27 250 7011/250 7541, info@kirururu.com Semi-permanent high quality safari camp.
Tarangire Treetops, tel: 2711 728 8818, res@halcyon hotels.com www.halcyon hotels.co.za For central book-ings tel: (0)27 250 0630-5. Part of the Elewana Africa chain of lodges, outside north-western boundary of park.

Mkomazi National Park
Babu's Camp, tel: (0)27 254 8840. Small, semi-permanent camp close to newly estab-lished park's headquarters.

Lushoto
Mullers Mountain Lodge, tel: (0)27 264 0204, elct_ned@tanga.net Former private house.
Grant's Lodge, tanga4@tanga.net www.grantslodge.com Former private house above Lushoto.
Lawns Hotel, Lushoto Town, tel: (0)27 264 0005/0076. Cheerful, reasonably priced.

WHERE TO EAT

Most tourists tend to eat in their hotels, except perhaps for lunch, but the following restaurants and cafés might be of interest.

Moshi
China Garden, cuisine as implied.
Chrisburgers, burgers etc.
El Rancho, good Indian food.
Indo-Italian Restaurant, cuisine as implied.
Salzburger Café, good value.

Arusha
The **TFA Shopping Centre** has several eating places includ-ing: **Chopstix** (Chinese), **Seafood Spot**, **Vama Indian Restaurant**, **Stiggbucks Coffee Bar**, **Msumbi Coffees**. Elsewhere in town are:

Bollate Restaurant, **Jambo Makuti**, **Khan's Grill**, **Mambo Jazz Café**, **Mc Moddy's**, **Matongee Club**, **Shangai Restaurant**, **Spices and Herbs**, **Stiggy's Restaurant**.

TOURS AND EXCURSIONS

There are various 'cultural tours' (escorted visits to tribal villages, etc.). Contact the Tanzania Tourist Board (*see* below) for details. These tours are often very worthwhile.

USEFUL CONTACTS

Arusha/Moshi Code: (0)27 **Arusha airport**, (0)27 250 5980; **Kilimanjaro Airport:** (0)27 275 4771; **Mt Meru Hospital:** (Arusha) (0)27 250 3352; **KCMC Hospital:** (Moshi) (0)27 275 4377; **AAR Arusha Medical Centre**, (0)27 250 1593; **AICC Hospital**, (0)27 254 4113; **Flying Doctor**, (0)27 250 2830; **Tanzania Tourist Board (Arusha)**, tel: (0)27 205 0025, culturaltourism@ habari.co.tz www. tanzaniatouristboard.com **Kilimanjaro NP HQ:** www.habari.co.tz/tanapa/ kilpakg.htm **Tanzania Tourist Board:** www.tanzania-web.com/home2.htm

KILIMANJARO	J	F	M	A	M	J	J	A	S	O	N	D
AVERAGE TEMP. °F	77	79	77	75	73	70	70	70	72	75	77	77
AVERAGE TEMP. °C	25	26	25	24	23	21	21	21	22	24	25	25
RAINFALL in	2	2	5	12	6	1	1	1	1	1	2	2
RAINFALL mm	39	44	117	303	157	31	14	14	15	33	55	48
DAYS OF RAINFALL	4	4	8	17	14	5	3	3	3	4	6	6

4
Ngorongoro and the Serengeti

Close to Tarangire, on the Arusha-Dodoma road, is the small settlement of **Makuyuni**, (Place of the Fig Tree). It is small and unprepossessing but it has significance. For the road which leads from it, across the **Rift Valley**, takes travellers through a sector of **Maasailand**, past **Lake Manyara** and its adjoining national park, up the steep western wall of the Rift and across the rolling, fertile **Mbulu Plateau**. Beyond rises **Ngorongoro**, encompassing its famous crater. And beyond Ngorongoro the track descends to the **Serengeti** plains through some of Africa's most superb scenery.

The world famous short-grass plains can be dusty and disappointingly 'empty' in the dry season. But from around mid-December to the beginning of June, with the grass green and the great migration making the most of it, the experience can be awesome. Great congregations of wildebeeste and zebra, soft-focused in the mists beneath Lemagrut, or flooding the plains between Naabi Hill and Ndutu, stagger the mind and senses.

THE RIFT VALLEY

The track which crosses the Rift from Makuyuni to Mto Wa Mbu (an interesting and enterprising town beneath the Rift's western wall) has recently been upgraded and tarred. Old Africa hands will wonder what the world is coming to, as the old track was straight out of Hell. As was, in a way, the Rift itself...which was formed as continental drift tore East Africa apart, dropping in a series of

CLIMATE

Daytime temperatures can rise quite high, even in Ngorongoro, but mean temperatures fall between 15°C (59°F) and 25°C (77°F). During the dry season (June to October) nights and early mornings can be cold enough for log fires to be lit in the lodges. Humidity is relatively low. The wettest months are usually March and April, when travel can sometimes be difficult on certain tracks.

Opposite: *Migrating wildebeest take the plunge at the Mara River.*

DON'T MISS

*** **Ngorongoro Crater:** world famous 'bowl' of wildlife. Best place to see rhino in Tanzania.
*** **Serengeti migration:** best in December and January, when the herds are in the southern plains and the weather is usually favourable (but see panel on page 74).
** **Lake Manyara National Park:** fine setting, with elephants, tree-climbing lions and flamingoes.
* **Olduvai Gorge:** site of Louis and Mary Leakeys' famous archeological finds.

blocks along parallel fault lines, resulting eventually in a system of irregular valleys, which stretches from the Dead Sea to Mozambique.

Parts of the Rift Valley, especially by Ol Doinyo Lengai, ('Mountain of God' to the Maasai) have a hard, spare beauty, founded on geological violence. Lengai itself remains violent – it rises, just outside the north-eastern corner of the Ngorongoro Conservation Unit in a steep cone to 2768m (9082ft). In 1966 it blew its main vent, spewing a plume of gas and cinders 1500m (5000ft) into the air, coating the mountain and the down-wind plains with caustic ash. It overlooks the bitter, alkaline waters of **Lake Natron**, a breeding ground of the lesser flamingo.

The Maasai

Opposite: *Once much feared, now much photographed – the proud and colourful warriors of Maasailand.*

The Rift is Maasai country. Tourists travelling down the road to Mto-Wa-Mbu, under the western Rift wall, will see the Maasai and their God-given cattle, as well as *enkang*, the circular arrangements of huts where the families and their cattle live. *Murran* (more commonly *moran*), the young warriors, live in their own *manyattas* elsewhere, with some of the *ndito* – the unmarried girls.

The Maasai have been much admired and romanticized. They are a fascinating people, many of whom cling to a traditional lifestyle. The men wear red blankets draped over their shoulders, carry spears or sticks and cover their hair and bodies with sheepfat and ochre. Livestock are central to their lives, and their diet still includes cow's blood

Ngorongoro and The Serengeti Area

mixed with milk. They appear to be at one with their environment, but life is still harsh: traditionally children often have two lower incisors knocked out to allow feeding in the event of lock-jaw, and male and female circumcision is still carried out without anaesthetic (*see* page 25). Maasai are not, however, unaffected by tourism, and tourists wanting to photograph them can expect to haggle for the privilege.

Lake Manyara National Park **

Mto Wa Mbu (Mosquito River) is well named, and well situated. The little settlement has become a popular stop-over for tourists and campers, providing them with souvenirs, fuel and basic groceries. Its population is ethnically mixed. Just beyond the township, to the south, is Lake Manyara National Park, between the lake and the Rift wall.

This 330km² (127 sq miles) park is known for its **elephants** and its **tree-climbing lions,** as well as the **flamingoes** and other fascinating **birds** which can be seen in impressive numbers on and around the shallow, alkaline lake. The area was once famous among big game hunters (one of them, Ernest Hemingway, describes it in *The Green Hills of Africa*). The elephant suffered drastically from the

MAASAI HUTS

Travellers across the Rift will see the circular *enkang* or family settlements of the Maasai, sometimes surrounded by a barrier of euphorbia or thorn trees, which keep cattle in and leopards and lions out. The low, loaf-shaped huts, built by the women from saplings and waterproof coverings of cow-dung are traditionally divided, by a screen, into two rooms, with a convoluted entrance hall between. Calves or goats are sometimes housed in this hallway at night. The main herds spend the night in the centre of the *enkang*, surrounded by their own little stockade. Each hut in an *enkang* has a special place, according to the status of its occupants.

THE LERAI FOREST

One of the most noticeable features of Ngorongoro Crater, when seen from the rim, is the Lerai Forest. Its name derives from the Maasai word for the yellow-bark acacia trees, which were once called 'fever trees' – a matter of guilt by association, for they grow in damp habitats, often alongside standing water, which of course is a wonderful breeding ground for the anopheles mosquito. The Lerai sometimes harbours bull elephant and waterbuck, but less than 30 years ago 23 rhino were resident in the forest, an amazing density of 7 rhino to the square kilometre (19 to the square mile). Other major features of the Crater include Lake Makat (the name means 'soda' in Maasai), the Mandusi and Gorigor swamps, and Engitate Hill.

highly organized poaching of the 1980s, but are now recovering. Other big game, including lion, is often seen, despite the fairly dense forest and bush. There are stretches of more open country by the lake.

Visitors often rush through Manyara's gloomy **groundwater forest,** the lovely *acacia tortilis* **woodland** and along the **soda flats** of its lake, before driving on to lunch at Ngorongoro. Yet Manyara has much to offer to those who can afford to stay for a day or more; one geologically interesting attraction are the **hot springs** at the far end of the park.

NGORONGORO CRATER

From Manyara the road makes a steep ascent up the Rift Wall (don't miss the fine views from the little lay-by near the top). The track then crosses the rolling **Mbulu Plateau**, rich farming country tilled by the Mbulu people (more properly the Iraqw). Beyond this lies the steep, thickly forested side of the Ngorongoro Crater, arguably the most famous wildlife refuge in the world. From the lodges on the crater rim, at about 2400m (8000ft), you look down upon the near-circular crater floor, an expanse of flat, open grassland, forest and lake 14km (9 miles) across. Around it stands a ring of extinct volcanoes with poetic Maasai names, and within the beautiful irregularity of the

Left: *Lake Makat (the Maasai word meaning soda) on the floor of Ngorongoro Crater.* **Opposite:** *A chance to relax by the swimming pool of Lake Manyara Hotel, overlooking the Rift Valley.*

bowl, something like 20,000 large or moderately large animals live out their lives. The crater (more accurately caldera) is a remarkable natural amphitheatre which properly takes its place as one of the essential highlights of East Africa.

The crater once belonged to the Maasai. In 1958 they signed away their right to live there, though they still take their cattle down to the soda-licks around Lake Makat. Sometimes they can be seen, striding across their old pastures with their herds, raising the dust of history as well as the volcanic soil. Red shukas streaming in the breeze, spears gleaming in the sun, they make a fine and moving sight.

Earlier in the 20th century the crater was occupied by German (and later British) farmers and squatters. In 1954 the squatters were evicted, and in 1959 the Conservation Area was inaugurated.

Visitors to Ngorongoro commonly arrive at one of the lodges after a day's trip from Arusha and Lake Manyara. The next morning they descend into the crater, 600m (2000ft) below, a volcanic basin where, despite the prevailing atmosphere of tranquillity, an abundance of animals jostle for a place in an intricately poised struggle for survival. In many ways the crater provides its tenants

FARMERS IN EDEN

In the early years of the 20th century two German brothers, **Friedrich and Adolph Siedentopf**, farmed the fabulous Ngorongoro Crater. The ruins of both farms can still be seen, one behind the Lerai Forest and the other across the crater on the slopes above the Munge Stream. They and their cattle shared the land with the **Maasai**, and of course some pretty eclectic farm animals, such as rhino and elephant. The Maasai, who believe that they own all the cattle in the world, sometimes 'claimed back' a few German beasts, and lion, which were often shot on sight as vermin, took a few more. The outbreak of World War I forced the brothers to leave Ngorongoro.

with their every need, but the rent in paradise can be very high, and is often paid in blood. Ngorongoro is not the open zoo that it sometimes seems to be; the animals are wild, and it is important to remember this.

The Wildlife

The number of **lion** on the crater floor varies, but is often around 100. Because of the nature of the crater, and the abundance of food, there is little pressure on the lions to move out, and much resistance to lions trying to move in. Consequently, many of Ngorongoro's lions are said to be closely related, which might (or might not) prove genetically damaging.

Lion are always popular, but the animal most tourists hope to to see in the crater is the **black rhino**, as Ngorongoro is one of the few places left in Africa where this much-persecuted creature can be seen in the wild. In the mid-1960s the biologist John Goddard recorded 110 rhinos on the crater floor. These were reduced to about 10 or 12 by the poaching epidemic of the 1980s. Since then, numbers in the crater have increased to about 20, thanks to more effective protection, though repopulation is slow, with gestation alone averaging 15 months.

Opposite: *A vehicle negotiates the steep and winding ascent road out of Ngorongoro Crater.*
Right: *A bull elephant reminds safari companies that he has right of way in Ngorongoro Crater.*

Another much-maligned animal in Ngorongoro is the **spotted hyena**. Like lion, hyena are largely active at night, and are great opportunists. Contrary to former opinion, however, they are very efficient hunters, and in Ngorongoro the image of the cowardly, skulking scavenger has been finally laid to rest. There are about eight clans living in Ngorongoro in their respective territories across the crater floor, each clan composed of 10 to 100 members. They are capable of keeping up a near-tireless, loping run, and of bringing down prey as large as adult wildebeest and zebra. Hyena kill about one quarter of all the new-born wildebeest in the crater each year, and are responsible for more overall kills than the lions, which, ironically, scavenge from the hyena.

Ngorongoro teems with other interesting species and in the crater there is rarely a dull moment. There seem to be animals everywhere – **elephant**, **wildebeest**, **zebra**, **buffalo**, **eland**, **Grant's** and **Thomson's gazelle**, **warthog** and many others, including the leggy and attractively spotted **serval cat** which patrols the taller grasslands, pouncing on mice or leaping from cover to claw birds from the air. The crater floor is perfect for **larks, longclaws**, **pipits** and **plovers**, as it is for the much larger **ostriches**, **Kori bustards** and the elegant **crowned cranes**.

NOT JUST THE CRATER

The Crater is only a small part of the Ngorongoro Conservation Area, 8300km² (3200 sq miles) in extent, and a unique experiment in multiple land-use. Its main features are the Crater Highlands (of which the famous crater is a small part) and the short-grass plains beyond, which merge with the vast grasslands of the adjacent Serengeti National Park.

Wildlife is protected throughout the area, with elephant, buffalo, leopard, bushbuck and a host of other animals being present, sometimes surprisingly close to the lodges on the crater's edge. Birds are abundant along the forested rim, and in and around the lodge gardens.

Above: *Olduvai Gorge, the site of many exciting palaentological discoveries.*

Olduvai Gorge *

Ngorongoro Crater has its share of archeological sites, and at least one splendid and sacred fig tree, said to have grown from the grave of a Barabaig warrior chief. But the track which passes between the crater rim and the slopes of Oldeani, the 'Mountain of Bamboo', then curves down towards the Serengeti, eventually crossing a slight but famous rocky gorge, where history has literally been laid bare.

In 1931 **Dr Louis Leakey**, following up previous explorations of Olduvai by a German professor, found human remains here. In 1959, after almost three decades of unrelenting work, Louis' wife **Mary** came running back to camp crying 'I've got him! I've got him!' The gentleman in question was nearly 2 million years old, and Mary had uncovered fragments of his skull. She named him 'Nutcracker Man' (*Australopithacus boisei*). Remains of 'Handy Man' (*Homo habilis*) – also about 1.8 million years old – were found later.

An even more exciting find came in 1976, when Mary Leakey discovered, in petrified volcanic ash at **Laetoli**, some 20km (12 miles) south of Olduvai, the clearly preserved footprints of three hominids. One was relatively large – though no more than 1.4m (4ft 7in), one medium-sized, and one small: perhaps a man, woman and child, if such terms are appropriate for hominids with a brain less than one third the size of our own. Whatever they were, they walked upright, and their stroll took place 3.5 million years ago.

There is a visitors' centre at Olduvai, with an interesting little museum and guided tours of the immediate gorge for those who choose to take them. Unless visitors are particularly interested, an hour in the vicinity is long enough.

SERENGETI NATIONAL PARK

Both Olduvai and Laetoli are on the edge of the Serengeti, 'The Great Open Place' to the Maasai. The Maasai lost the Serengeti, along with Ngorongoro, when the areas were made into National Parks, but at places such as the Bell Rock at **Moru Kopjes**, where the impact of a large rock being struck by smaller ones rings out across the great plains, there is evidence of the warriors' passing. Rangers will tell you that the *Il murran* would strike the rock to guide their cattle-raiding comrades home, but knowing the warriors, they probably did it just to amuse themselves. There is a cave on another nearby kopje, with Maasai rock-paintings (relatively recent) by its entrance, depicting shields and figures.

SERENGETI KOPJES

Kopje (pronounced copy) is a Dutch word meaning small hill. The Serengeti kopjes consist of old granite rock, broken and worn by constant expansion and contraction due to abrupt temperature changes. Like oceanic islands, they have their own range of vegetation and wildlife, and are often home to lizards, hyrax and those delightful antelopes, the dik-dik. Snakes such as the spitting cobra and puff adder are sometimes found there, as are klipspringer antelope, lion and leopard. Close to the Naabi Hill–Seronera track and about 10km (6 miles) to the southeast of Seronera are the Simba Kopjes, always worth a visit, as are the Maasai Kopjes near Seronera itself. The Moru Kopjes are some 30km (20 miles) south of Seronera, and a pleasant place to spend the day, and enjoy a picnic lunch, or even camp.

Left: *Plain sailing – a balloon drifts silently over the short-grass savanna of the Serengeti.*

BLACK-MANED LIONS

Male lions in Ngorongoro and the Serengeti often have beautiful black manes, once much-prized by hunters. As a leonine means of showing off, bushy black manes, like bushy black beards, have their advantages, but when hunting on open grassland, an approaching black haystack must look as obvious, to a wildebeest or zebra, as a London taxi. Which might explain why female lions everywhere do most of the hunting and why, especially in the Crater, most lion scavenge from hyena in any case.

Kopjes – outcrops of granite rock – rise like shimmering islands in the Serengeti's sea of grass, and are a most attractive feature of the Park. One of them, **Naabi Hill,** marks the major gate of the Serengeti, commanding the most beautiful acacia and short-grass savanna, the plains sweeping away on every hand as if to challenge the concept of the horizon.

Big Cats

Much of the southern Serengeti is ideal cheetah habitat, especially by the Gol Kopjes, where there is firm, open space, often lots of Thomson's and Grant's gazelles (the cheetah's preferred prey) and suitable cover among the longer turfts of grass. The leggy supermodels of the cat world are in their element here.

Lions enjoy the Serengeti too, as one might expect in what for them must seem like the biggest supermarket on earth, with no-one manning the tills. And that other charismatic and exquisite feline, the **leopard**, is common, though not always commonly seen. More nocturnal and shy than lions and cheetahs, the leopard can sometimes be found along the Seronera Valley, in the centre of the Park, or along other watercourses, resting in trees or among kopjes. If you are lucky enough to see one, don't spoil your observations or photo-opportunities by sudden movements or noises.

Left: *Wildebeest hard at work mowing the Serengeti plains.*
Opposite: *A female cheetah with four young mouths to feed, scans the Musiara Plains.*

The Serengeti Migration

For the resident lion and spotted hyena, however, life is largely feast or famine, as the convenience food on which they rely so much, wildebeest and zebra, have a disconcerting habit of disappearing. However, what is frustrating for the cats is pure theatre for tourists, and the Serengeti migration can well claim to be the greatest wildlife show on Earth.

Involving huge numbers of animals in a spectacular landscape, the migration is, at its best, almost overwhelming in its visual and emotional impact. The sanctuary in which it takes place is an enormous 14,763km² (5700 sq miles) in area, as big as Northern Ireland. It is adjoined by the **Masai Mara** across the border, **Maswa Game Reserve** to the west, and the **Ngorongoro Conservation Area** to the southeast. Two smaller game reserves, Grumeti and Ikorongo, now developed for tourism, lie to the northwest. Even by African standards, this is game country on a vast scale.

The animals involved in the migration move because they need to eat. Two million or more herbivores need a great amount of grass, and in the long dry season, from

MIGRATION FACT FILE

• As many as 1,500,000 wildebeest and 200,000 zebra take part, augmented by throngs of semi-migratory Thomson's gazelle, eland, topi and hartebeest. There can be densities of 500 wildebeest per square kilometre.
• To add to the turmoil, the beginning of the trek, in May or June, coincides with the wildebeest rutting period.
• The herds are constantly under threat from a variety of predators, including 1500 lion, 4000 hyena, 500 cheetah, as well as leopard and (in the Grumeti River) giant crocodiles. Many hyena actually commute, for distances of up to 60km (40 miles) or more, from their home bases, to find prey.
• In length, the journey from the short-grass plains and back again is 800km (500 miles).

WHEN TO SEE THE MIGRATION

The migration's most spectacular phase usually takes place in late May / early June, when the great herds stream north from the short-grass plains. Lake Ndutu Lodge is often perfectly placed for this. Other lodges that might be appropriate then include the Serena, Sopa and Seronera. June/July, when the herds cross the Grumeti River, is also a prime time at Grumeti, Kirawira, Sasakwa Hill, Sabora and Faru Faru. The Western Corridor and Northern Serengeti come into their own from Jun–Nov, when Klein's Camp, Loliondo Camp and Lobo Lodge are well positioned. From around mid-November to late May the migration returns south, when Ndutu Lodge, Olduvai Gorge Camp and the Ngorongoro Crater lodges are worth considering.

May to November, the short-grass plains to the south and southeast of Seronera are dessicated (and in any case shorn as short as suburban lawns by two million sets of incisors). So at the end of May or in early June (the timing varies, depending on the rains) the greatest natural circus in the world gets on the road. Its performers move out in files which can be 40km (25 miles) long, and the short-grass plains are sometimes virtually emptied of migratory animals within three or four days. It is this brief and unpredictable exodus which is so often filmed and photographed by those who are lucky enough to be around at the time.

The herds are followed, at least for some of the way, by the more nomadic predators – certain lions, hyenas and jackals. The long journey also takes the migrant herds through the home ranges of prides of lion and packs of hyena, and across rivers, such as the **Grumeti** and the **Mara**, where monstrous crocodiles lie in wait, to fling themselves upon drinking animals or twist great chunks from the corpses of those that drown.

The hazardous journey takes the herds out into the **Western Corridor** of the Serengeti, then far beyond the Kenyan border, before returning to the southern plains. It is a triangular trek of about 800km (500 miles) which some

wildebeest will complete many times before disease or predators catch up with them, a testimony to their toughness. Surprisingly, however, an adult wildebeest can be brought down by a lion, or even a single hyena, with scarcely a groan of protest, despite its size and its horns, although a female will often successfully defend her young ones against similar attacks.

The **return** to the short-grass plains is timed to coincide with the Short Rains in December, and with the short and synchronized calving season which usually begins in January. Sometimes they (or the Gods) get it wrong: if the rains come late, or not at all, up to 80% of the new calves die due to lack of food. When they get it right, the scenes on the short-grass, with hundreds of thousands of animals scattered

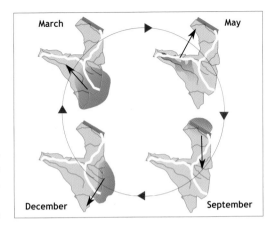

THE SERENGETI WILDEBEEST MIGRATION CYCLE

across a whole landscape, and the calves skipping, running and bleating with apparent *joie de vivre*, are almost as spectacular as the exodus in May or June. And, of course, the timing is more convenient for tourists.

The wildebeests' travelling companions include large numbers of their antelope cousins, the **topi** and the **hartebeest** (*kongoni*). Their hind legs, shorter than the fore, act like low gears, to give them maximum acceleration from a standing start, and once on the move they are soon in overdrive. They are among the fastest of herbivores and, despite their ungainly shape, quite attractive.

Smaller Animals

One of the Serengeti's more interesting residents is the **honey-badger** – loose-skinned, powerfully jawed and, when aroused, utterly fearless. Their silver-grey and black coloration is for warning, not for camouflage, and honey-badgers (sometimes called *ratels*) will attack animals as large as buffalo, biting the prey's groin and genital organs and leaving the animal to bleed to death. Tourists need not walk around in body armour, however, although the honey-badger has been known to attack car tyres.

Opposite: *A resting leopard lounges in the limbs of an acacia.*

DEFENDING WILDEBEEST

Wildebeest are not the clowns of the plains they are sometimes said to be. Nature hasn't blessed them with a high IQ but they are otherwise well-adapted to a lifestyle which, in human terms, no insurance company would touch. A calf can stand almost as soon as it is born, and within an average time of seven minutes is able to run, albeit unsteadily, for its life. With a range of hungry predators on their tail, such precocity is very much in their interest. The wildebeest's lawnmower of a mouth is superbly designed to harvest grass – which is why they eat themselves out of house and home twice a year, and why they migrate.

Right: *A klipspringer, the 'Goat of the Rocks', watches the world from a Serengeti kopje.*
Opposite: *Thompson's gazelle, distinguished by a black side stripe, on the Serengeti plains.*

Other smaller mammals of the Serengeti include the **black** or **silver-backed jackal**, **golden jackal**, **bat-eared fox**, **genet** (often to be seen around Ndutu Lodge), six species of **mongoose** and the skunk-like **zorilla**. Altogether there are almost 100 species of mammal found in the Park, and nearly 500 **birds**. Ground-nesting birds are abundant in the short-grass plains, as are the storks, vultures, eagles, hawks and falcons which thrive on the prodigality of the grasslands.

Around the Park

The short-grass plains of the southeastern Serengeti phase into an intermediate zone by **Naabi Hill**, and into long-grass plains closer to **Seronera**, where a lodge, a research institute and a visitors' centre are situated. About 18km (11 miles) north of Seronera is Banagi, and just to the east of here is **Kilimafedha**, the 'Hill of Wealth', so-called because gold was mined here until 1966. The gold-bearing quartz is embedded in some of the most ancient rock on Earth, found between Banagi and Kilimafedha, and some two to three thousand million years old. The Serengeti is not short on superlatives.

SWEET-TALKING BIRD

The myopic and misanthropic honey-badger has a remarkable relationship with the honey guide (the Latin name of which is – appropriately – *Indicator indicator*). The honey guide is a small bird which attracts the badger (and human honey-hunters) to wild bees' nests by its behaviour and calls. The badger then digs out the nest, and bird and mammal share the spoils. The bird gets the best of the deal – the honey-badger is, in fact, quite capable of finding its own hives.

Towards **Banagi**, and further northwards towards the Kenyan border, the country lifts into rolling uplands, fledged with bush and patchy woodland, relieved by open areas and ranges of hills. Many of the hills have crumbled into magnificent kopjes. The countryside in this vicinity is a joy to both eye and soul, and from August to November part of the great wildlife migration passes through, adding spectacle to splendour. Various lodges, as in other sectors of the park, are strategically situated in these areas. (*See* fact panel, page 74.)

Similarly well-placed lodges serve the **Western Corridor**, a tapering arm of the park which stretches to **Ndabaka Gate**, overlooking the shores of Lake Victoria. It is at its best, as far as game viewing is concerned, during the dry season from June to October. This is also the best time for travelling, as there are extensive black-cotton grasslands 30km (20 miles) east of Ndabaka. Black-cotton soil can be a nightmare during the rains, even for experienced off-the-road drivers in four-wheel-drive vehicles, and in the bush, discretion is almost always the better part of valour.

GRUMETI RIVER

The main feature of the Western Corridor is the Grumeti River, which flows through the Corridor from east to west, and empties into Lake Victoria. Exceptionally large crocodiles live in this river, and visitors are advised not to stand or walk too close to the water's edge, for the huge reptiles are capable of surging from the river to grab unsuspecting wildebeest (or unsuspecting tourists). The less violent and extremely attractive colobus monkey lives in the canopy of the riverine forest, and that other magnificent black and white creature, the martial eagle, can sometimes be seen in the area.

Ngorongoro and the Serengeti at a Glance

The long rains (mid-March to mid-May) and to a lesser extent the short rains (mid-October to mid-December) can cause certain tracks to become difficult or impassable but can be rewarding. Mid-May to mid-October generally dry and (late afternoon until mid-morning) pleasantly cool, even cold in the highlands.

Most visitors arrive by chartered aircraft or safari company vehicle, via Arusha. Arusha is the main stopover for travellers coming by long-distance buses or safari company vehicles from Dar es Salaam, Nairobi (Kenya) or Mombasa (Kenya).

Transport in and around the northern parks is almost entirely by safari company or private vehicles, operating out of or via Arusha. There is also a cheap and cheerful Ngorongoro shuttle bus connecting Arusha with Ngorongoro.

Lake Manyara Area
Lake Manyara Hotel, central reservations tel: (0)27 254 4595. Longest-established of all Manyara hotels/lodges in superb location overlooking park and lake.
Lake Manyara Serena, tel: (Arusha) (0)27 253 9161/313 and 253 9160 reservations@serena.co.tz Luxury lodge, Rift Valley escarpment. Splendid views.
Maji Moto Luxury Camp, central reservations (0)27 254 8078, information@conscorp.co.za www.ccafrica.com Furthest corner of Lake Manyara NP, between lake and Rift wall.
Lake Natron Camp, central reservations tel: (0)27 255 3638, www.safaris-tz.com Simple camp between active volcano, Ol Donyo Lengai (climbs arranged), and Lake Natron.

Ngorongoro Area
Ngorongoro Crater Lodge, central reservations (0)27 254 8078. High-end luxury lodge in prime location on southern rim of Crater.
Ngorongoro Wildlife Lodge, on edge of Crater, central reservations, tel: (0)27 254 4595. Former state-owned lodge, now in private hands.
Ngorongoro Sopa Lodge, tel: (0)27 250 0630-9, info@sopalodges.com www.sopalodges.com Well-appointed lodge, fine views.
Ngorongoro Serena Safari Lodge, tel: (0)27 253 7050/7052/7053/7055. Luxury lodge with wonderful views.
Gibbs Farm, tel: (Arusha) (0)27 253 4302, www.gibbsfarm.net Old coffee farm, on slopes of Ngorongoro, at Karatu.
Plantation Lodge, tel: (0)27 254 4360. Small, personal lodge amid lovely scenery near Karatu, on coffee estate. Outstanding cuisine.

Serengeti (South/Central)
Ndutu Safari Lodge, details as in Ngorongoro section. Lodge is on boundary between Ngorongoro and Serengeti.
Seronera Serena Safari Lodge, tel: (0)27 262 1519/1507. Built on hilltop overlooking plains on one of main migration routes.
Serengeti Sopa, tel: (Arusha) (0)27 250 0630-34/36, info@sopalodges.com www.sopalodges.com Excellent game viewing.
Kusini Camp, tel: (0)27 250 9817, info@kerdowney.com Small, personal tented camp, southwest Serengeti. Best from mid-December–March though game never far away.
Serengeti Wilderness Camp, central reservations tel: (0)27 11 702 2035. Small, seasonal, eco-friendly camp in heart of the park.
Seronera Wildlife Lodge, central reservations tel: (0)27 254 4595. Excellent position by Seronera Valley.

Serengeti (Western Corridor)
Faru Faru Lodge, central bookings (0)27 262 2074. Intimate lodge overlooking waterhole and Grumeti River. Part of Singita Grumeti Reserves group.
Kirawira Camp, tel: (0)28 262 1518. Part of well-respected Serena Group, luxury tented camp on slopes overlooking Grumeti River Valley.
Mbalageti Serengeti Lodge, central reservations tel: (0)27

Ngorongoro and the Serengeti at a Glance

254 8632. Located on hilltop, off the beaten track in Western Corridor.
Sabora Tented Camp, central bookings (0)28 262 2074. Part of the Singita Grumeti Reserves group. 1920s theme luxury camp on the plains of the Grumeti Reserves.
Sasakwa Lodge, central bookings (0)28 262 2074. Part of Singita Grumeti Reserves group. Situated on plateau alongside Western Corridor, built in the style of an expansive 1920s manor house.
Grumeti River Camp, tel: (0)27 254 8549, information@conscorp.co.za www.ccafrica.com Exclusive tented camp in 'Western Corridor'. Good all year but particularly exciting in June when migration braves adjacent Grumeti River and its giant crocodiles.
Kijereshi Tented Camp, tel: (0)27 250 0517/0617. Situated in Kijereshi Game Reserve on border of Western Corridor.

Serengeti (North)
Serengeti Migration Camp, central booking tel: (0)27 250 0630. Part of Elewana Africa group. Northern corner of Serengeti, on Grumeti River and a main migratory route.
Lobo Wildlife Lodge, central reservations tel: (0)27 254 4595. Long-established, creatively designed lodge built into a granite outcrop with exquisite views over prime big game country.

Klein's Camp, central reservations, tel: (0)27 254 8078, information@conscorp.co.za www.ccafrica.com Exclusive camp amid Kuka Hills outside northeastern boundary of Serengeti. Best in November when migration usually passes through, but resident game all year.
Mbuzi Mawe, tel: (0)28 262 2040/2042. Luxury camp, part of Serena Group, situated on rocky outcrop in beautifully scenic Lobo area.
Nduara Loliondo Camp, no direct bookings, but Nomad's (the owning group) tel: (0)27 255 3819, cell: (0)784 734 490. Exclusive mobile camp. Moves twice a year to follow migration through Loliondo area to east of park.

WHERE TO EAT

Almost everyone eats in their lodges or safari camps, where the food is often excellent.

TOURS AND EXCURSIONS

Empakai Crater/Lengai: There are now several popular guided hiking/camping treks in the Ngorongoro Conservation Area, to interesting places such as Empakai and the active volcano Ol Donyo Lengai, which

trekkers can climb if they wish.
Olduvai Gorge: This is another interesting diversion, just a short drive from Ngorongoro – Serengeti track. Historic site of Ancient Man, with a small museum.
Balloon Safaris: Operated from Seronera and other lodges. Champagne breakfast served on landing.
There are various 'cultural tours' (escorted visits to tribal villages, etc.) available in these areas. Contact the Tanzania Tourist Board (see below) for details. These tours are often very interesting and worthwhile.

USEFUL CONTACTS

Arusha/Moshi code: (0)27
Kilimanjaro Airport: (0)27 275 4771
Mt Meru Hospital: (Arusha) (0)27 250 3352
Flying Doctor: (0)27 250 2830
Ngorongoro Crater: www.ngorongoro-crater-africa.org
Serengeti NP: www.serengetipark.org
Tanzania Tourist Board (Arusha), tel: (0)27 205 0025, cell: (0)754 420 258, cultural tourism@habari.co.tz www.tanzaniatouristboard.com

NGORONGORO	J	F	M	A	M	J	J	A	S	O	N	D
AVERAGE TEMP. °F	70	70	70	70	66	63	63	64	66	68	70	70
AVERAGE TEMP. °C	21	21	21	21	19	17	17	18	19	20	21	21
RAINFALL in	3	3	5	10	3	1	0	0	0	1	4	4
RAINFALL mm	74	85	139	245	78	18	9	7	10	20	107	96
DAYS OF RAINFALL	9	9	13	21	13	4	3	2	2	2	10	11

5
The Lakes

It is difficult for most of us today to appreciate the fascination which the 'question of the Nile' held for the geographers, politicians and the better-informed general public of Victorian Britain. Explorers and missionaries tramped westwards from the east coast of Africa to the Lakes in search of the source of the sacred river and, perhaps, some kind of immortality. They mostly found mortality. Even Livingstone was brought to his knees, and an early death, in the swamps of Bangweulu (now in northern Zambia), hopelessly seduced by the search for those elusive headwaters. And the man who finally solved the nagging question, John Hanning Speke, shot himself soon afterwards and is now almost forgotten.

Speke revealed that the Nile flows from the lake still called Victoria, though modern geographers have recently discovered a 'new' source northeast of Lake Tanganyika. Known by the Luo people of Kenya as *Nam Lolwe*, 'Lake Without End', Victoria is almost 70,000km² (27,000 sq miles) in area, the biggest lake in Africa and the second largest in the world.

Tanzania shares Lake Victoria with Kenya and Uganda, and **Lake Tanganyika**, 320km (200 miles) to the southwest, with Zaïre. Tanganyika, unlike Victoria, is a Rift Valley lake, and at more than 1433m (4700ft) is the second deepest in the world. It is also the world's longest freshwater lake. In the southwestern corner of the country is the third great lake, **Malawi**. Shared with both Malawi and Mozambique, it is another Rift Valley lake, overlooked by the magnificent Livingstone Mountains.

CLIMATE

The climate around the Lakes is very similar, in some respects, to that at the coast. The atmosphere can be oppressively hot and humid during the single rainy season, from the beginning of November to end of April, but generally the lakes themselves have a cooling effect, and temperatures are normally pleasant and constant. Minimum temperatures at Mwanza throughout the year are about 17°C (62°F) with maximums of 28°C (82°F).

Opposite: *Canoes on Lake Tanganyika, a ready way to sell fresh produce.*

Below: *The pleasant town of Mwanza, on the shores of Lake Victoria.*

LAKE VICTORIA

John Speke first saw the lake he was to call Victoria on 3 August 1858, from a point where the town of **Mwanza** now stands. Speke was wondrously confident that he was looking at the lake which fed the Nile, and in memory of his momentous sighting the inlet he had been standing beside was later named Speke's Gulf.

The country through which he had marched from **Kazeh**, close to present-day **Tabora**, is largely unremarkable until the traveller approaches the lake, when the monotonous landscape is transformed into sweeping, almost treeless plains which are studded, like the Serengeti, with islands of granite. The air grows more humid and the land greener, for Victoria has its own micro-climate, and moods. Its shallow, normally placid waters tend to reflect the hues of the sky, and during storms its colour can almost match the blackness of its temper. On calm, fine days it glitters with a scintillating blueness, and its sunsets, from the eastern shores, can be astonishing in their reflected intensity. The writer Alan Moorehead has said that such scenes 'are very beautiful, and yet there is a mysterious and disturbing atmosphere about the lake. One feels here very strongly the primitiveness of Africa, its overwhelming multiplicity in emptiness'.

Mwanza *

Mwanza, on Lake Victoria's southeastern corner, is a pleasant enough place, especially along its waterfront, where several tourist-class hotels are becoming established. For those who just want to relax, its air of unreproving indolence, broken only by the cries of the hadada ibis which roosts in the lakeside trees, can be a virtue in itself.

Lake Victoria and Lake Tanganyika Area

**THE AMPHIBIOUS
SITATUNGA**

The sitatunga resembles a long-legged bushbuck, but with fairly long, shaggy hair which is slightly oily, enabling them to spend much of their time in the water, or even completely immersed when threatened. Their splayed hooves allow them to step more easily across spongy mats of vegetation. On dry land, however, the hooves are something of a hindrance, making the animal more vulnerable to predators or hunters, though the sitatunga, like the bushbuck, will defend itself courageously against attackers, including men and dogs.

Below: The prominent but precarious Bismarck Rock in Mwanza harbour.

Mwanza's economy in recent years, apart from the fishing industry, has largely depended upon the agricultural produce of its fertile hinterland, farmed by the dominant tribe of the area, the **Sukuma**. The Sukuma are growers of cotton, maize and cassava, and they also herd cattle, although coffee shipped through the port originates in the West Lake Province, across the waters.

It is just a short ferry trip from Mwanza to **Saa Nane** (Two O'Clock) Island. Its small wildlife sanctuary badly needs upgrading but the island itself is quite attractive and worth a visit. Mwanza's best-known landmark, **Bismarck Rock**, can be seen from the nearby shore, to the west of the town.

Rubondo *

In the southwestern corner of Lake Victoria is a most delightful and unusual national park, Rubondo Island. Accessible by air (and sometimes by sea) from Mwanza, it is well worth the air charter prices or the longish boat journey. Its humid forest and wetland ecosystems are home to a number of indigenous species, such as the otherwise rarely encountered, semi-aquatic sitatunga, marsh mongooses and genet. There are also a few introduced animals, such as chimpanzees, roan antelope, giraffe and elephants. Plans to turn it into a sanctuary for black rhinos have so far been unsuccessful. It boasts an impressive variety of birds, some brilliantly varied butterflies, and among its array of beautiful plants are ground and tree orchids, fireball lilies which flower during the short rains, and the red coral tree which blossoms for most of the year. A simple but wonderfully situated little camp, ideal for honeymooners, occupies a clearing on the lakeshore, near the island's centre.

Left: *Lake Victoria is an inland sea. Substantial ferries such as this one docked at Mwanza are used for inter-lake connections.*

Bukoba *

The overlap between East and West Africa is a distinguishing characteristic of the West Lake Province, and a pleasant way of appreciating it is to sail from Mwanza to Bukoba, the western province's major town, on one of the Lake ferries. The Kagera region lies between the lake and Rwanda and Burundi, with Uganda to the north. It is considered, by some, to be the most attractive part of Tanzania.

Bukoba (founded by the ill-fated but brilliant eccentric, Emin Pasha) is situated on the lower slopes of the hills which overlook the lake. Rarely visited by tourists, it has an attractive location and restful atmosphere. Its hotels will never figure in the world's top ten but the best of them have a certain rural charm.

The people of Bukoba and of Kagera Region in general are **Haya**. Mostly Ugandan in origin, they are said to take quick advantage of formal education, though most of them are farmers, growing Robusta coffee, maize, beans, sweet potatoes and bananas. Like the Chagga, they have adopted the banana as their staple diet – they often eat them roasted, and served on banana leaves, accompanied by banana wine, which they sip through straws of grass.

Despite its remoteness, Bukoba has seen its share of action, defended by the Germans in World War I, and inaccurately bombed during Idi Amin's ill-fated incursions into Tanzania during the late 1970s.

BUKOBA'S WILDLIFE

Bukoba's westerly position is reflected in some of the bird species found there and in the adjacent region. Exciting species include:
- **Grey parrot:** the familiar talking parrot.
- **Ross's turaco**.
- **Eastern grey plantain eater:** which, of course, lives on bananas.
- **Northern brown-throated weaver:** often seen in the garden of the Lake Hotel.
- Anyone walking by the lakeside might be also be rewarded by the sight of **spotted-necked otters**, which will sometimes fish and frolic close to the shore in the clear blue waters of the lake.

STANLEY AND LIVINGSTONE

After two decades of determined exploring deep into Africa, David Livingstone was a well-known figure throughout the English-speaking world. Some deserters from his 1866 expedition past Lake Nyasa spread a rumour that he was dead, precipitating a search not resolved until Stanley, working for the *New York Times*, presumed to meet him under a mango tree in Ujiji. Stanley, who had dressed for the occasion and was very nervous (he half expected to be rebuffed), was later asked if he had actually uttered the famous phrase. 'Yes', he replied, 'I couldn't think what else to say.' The two got on well, explored regions of Lake Tanganyika together, and were said to have wept when they parted months later.

Below: *The Mahale mountains, home of chimpanzees, rising from the shores of Lake Tanganyika.*

Lake Tanganyika

Lake Tanganyika is one of the most interesting lakes in the world. The combination of antiquity (the dead 'fossil water' of its profound depths may be 20 million years old) and its isolation have produced many unique life forms. Most of the 250 species of fish which inhabit its rich upper waters are endemic, including many colourful cichlids, and a whole range of gastropods, molluscs and crustaceans. It even has a unique water snake, the Eastern aquatic cobra, which fishes by day and sleeps on the rocks by night. More aesthetically, Tanganyika often provides superb sunsets.

Ujiji *

If the waters of Tanganyika are filled with fascination, its shores are no less so. The topography to the east is largely monotonous, though **Henry Morton Stanley** 'regarded the alluring face of the land with a fatuous love'. Ujiji was the spot where Stanley finally caught up with **David Livingstone**, asking his famous question under a mango tree, which has now been replaced by a rather less attractive memorial. Ujiji's more general past, as an important terminus of the caravan route from the coast, is evident in the Arabic influences of Swahili-style houses, some with carved doors, and in a predominantly Muslim population. The town is quite large and spaciously laid out, and the shallow creek which passes for its harbour quite picturesque.

Kigoma *

Ujiji's importance declined with the ending of the slave and ivory trade, and it is now a satellite of Kigoma, 10km (6 miles) to the north. Kigoma came into prominence for the same reason as Ujiji – as the terminus of a trade route from the coast – although in Kigoma's case communications are by rail and the passengers leaving for the coast are not slaves. The **railway** was completed by the Germans in 1914, and soon afterwards appropriated by the British. For those who like to travel in style, it is not the best way to get to Kigoma, as the trip from Dar takes two days and is not the last word in comfort. But it beats walking all the way, as the explorers did.

Kigoma is a quiet town though its population and that of surrounding areas have been swollen by refugees from the Congo DR and Burundi. Its principle street slopes up from the interesting old station between mangoes and frangipani. Kigoma's main attraction is its lakeside location, and its role as a base for Mahale and Gombe chimpanzee sanctuaries.

Mahale Mountains National Park **

One of the destinations of the *Liemba* is **Magambo**, 115km (70 miles) south of Kigoma. Passengers travel from ferry to shore by small boat. Another boat then takes them to **Kasongo**, the headquarters of Mahale Mountains National Park. The complete trip from Kigoma takes about nine hours, and must be well planned and co-ordinated. Speedboats operate from the Hilltop Hotel in Kigoma, taking three to four hours, but are quite expensive. There are three luxury camps by the lake. Cheaper alternatives include a basic, self-catering rest-house and camping facilities, but these should be booked in advance through the park authorities.

However, travellers should not be put off. Mahale Mountains is a delightful sanctuary, its lovely montane topography, draped in rainforest and inhabited by chimpanzees and other primates, with lower orders of animals, including birds and insects, being well represented.

Sunsets across the lake, and the fascinating lake itself, add to Mahale's isolated charms.

M.V. LIEMBA

Kigoma's most famous boat is an old lady with an interesting past: assembled from pre-fabricated sections at the start of World War I, she was fitted out with a 4.1 gun taken from the sunken battle-cruiser *Koenigsberg* and made ready for action. When the action came, however, the *Graf von Goetzen* (as she was then known) was sent to the bottom by a Belgian bomb. The British salvaged her in 1924, and after an extensive refit she was pressed back in service. She is still going strong, ferrying passengers to different parts of Lake Tanganyika.

IS THIS A *DAGAA* I SEE BEFORE ME?

On moonless nights, while Lake Tanganyika's amazing aquatic cobra catches up on its sleep on the rocks by the shore, local fishermen of the Ha tribe sail out in little boats in search of shoals of *dagaa*, the small, sardine-like fish which, after being sun-dried, provides a cheap and essential protein for the lakeside people, and for many other people throughout Tanzania (they can often be seen in markets far from the Lakes). The *dagaa* are attracted to lights suspended from the boats, then panicked into stillness by a sudden beating of drums, before being hoisted up into scoop nets.

Gombe Stream National Park ★★★

Gombe Stream, much closer to Kigoma and much smaller than Mahale, is similarly beautiful, though it has become isolated as surrounding forests have been destroyed. Only 25km (15 miles) north of Kigoma, it is accessible by boat. Water taxis operate from Kigoma, taking four to six hours. Speedboats take less than an hour.

Gombe's montane forests are famous for their chimpanzees, though like Mahale it contains many other species of animals. The chimpanzees have been studied for decades by many observers, most famous of whom is **Dr Jane Goodall**. She has been connected with Gombe since 1960 and much of the credit for the studies there must go to her. Gombe has a small rest house, but basically visitors have to be self-sufficient. Camping is possible by the shore.

Katavi Plains National Park ★

One of Tanzania's most remote and least-visited sanctuaries, Katavi is most easily accessed by air. By road (from Dar via Mbeya and Sumbawanga), the journey presently

Left: *The flame of the Independence Monument adds warmth to the cool mountain air of Mbeya.*
Opposite: *A chimpanzee, a primate found in both Mahale Mountains and Gombe Stream national parks on the shores of Lake Tanganyika.*

takes at least four days, so this is not a safari for the unadventurous. But the rewards are enormous, for Katavi's miombo woodland and long-grass plains are home to an impressive number of animals and birds. And the chances are that you'll have this chunk of 'real Africa' all to yourself. There are three small luxury camps, but independent campers need to be particularly self-sufficient.

THE SOUTHWEST
Mbeya *

Travellers to Mbeya – 900km (550 miles) southwest of Dar, will be tempted to stay. The town is small, and has little to offer tourists but relative peace and quiet but its location, among lovely mountain ranges, and its correspondingly cool climate, endear it to expatriates and travellers. There are a number of very pleasant walks in the hills, and a short drive away is Tanzania's smallest and newest national park, known locally as 'Bustari ya Mungu', the 'Garden of God'. From around Christmas until May the area, on the Kitulo Plateau, is a profusion of orchids and other flowers. Mbeya is also a good base from which to explore the lovely northern shores of Lake Malawi.

Lake Malawi *

Last and smallest of Tanzania's Great Lakes is Malawi, sometimes known as Lake Nyasa. It is too far from the main tourist haunts to be regarded as a popular destination, but travellers to or from the south, who have the time to drive the extra 130km (80 miles) from Mbeya to the small port of **Itungi**, might be glad they have made the journey. Like Lake Tanganyika, Malawi is exceptionally rich in endemic species of fish and other water creatures. The scenery, with the **Livingstone Mountains** rising high above the head of the lake, is quite splendid, especially when seen from a boat.

Above: *A fisherman's canoe beached on the shores of beautiful Lake Malawi.*
Right: *Lake Malawi fishermen mending their nets by the shores of the great lake.*

The Lakes at a Glance

BEST TIMES TO VISIT

Rains (peaking Nov–Dec and Mar–Apr) can be dismal. Mid-May to mid-October is much drier and (in mornings and evenings) pleasantly cool.

GETTING THERE

Road and rail journeys to the Lakes are not recommended unless you don't mind delays and discomfort.

GETTING AROUND

Taxis are available in main towns. There are a few travel companies in Mwanza and Kigoma. Chartered flights are available and there are regular ferries to various destinations on Lakes Victoria and Tanganyika.

WHERE TO STAY

Lake Victoria
MWANZA
Tilapia, tel: (Mwanza) (0)28 250 0517/250 0617, tilapia@mwanza.com Upper end, pleasant, popular. Prime location on Lake Victoria.
New Mwanza Hotel, (0)28 250 1070. Long-established upper-end hotel in town.
Speke Bay Lodge, tel: (0)28 262 1236. Upper-end hotel 15 km south of Serengeti's Ndabaka Gate.

RUBONDO ISLAND NATIONAL PARK
Rubondo Island Camp, tel: (0)27 250 8790. On lovely, secluded little bay in the southwestern corner of Lake Victoria.

Lake Tanganyika
KIGOMA
Kigoma Hilltop, central reservations (Chimpanzee Safaris) tel: (0)22 213 0553, cell (0)713 620 154. Large, well-appointed hotel on hillside by Lake Tanganyika.

Accommodation in Parks
GOMBE STREAM
Gombe Tented Camp, central reservations (Chimpanzee Safaris) tel: (0)22 213 0553, cell (0)713 620 154. Only alternative accommodation is a simple rest house or camping.

KATAVI PLAINS NATIONAL PARK
Chada Katavi, no direct bookings, but Nomad's (the owning group) tel: (0)27 255 3819, cell: (0)784 734 490.
Fox's Katavi Wildlife Camp, central reservations tel: (0)22 286 357, cell: (0)713 237 422/(0)754 237 422/(0)784 237 422. Simple, hospitable camp at edge of woodland.

MAHALE MOUNTAINS
Greystoke Mahale, no direct bookings, but Nomad's tel: (0)27 255 3819, cell: (0)784 734 490. Exclusive camp by shores of Lake Tanganyika.

Nkugwe Tented Camp, central reservations (Chimpanzee Safaris) tel: (0)22 213 0553, cell (0)713 620 154. Lakeside luxury camp.

WHERE TO EAT

Mwanza's restaurants include: **Rock Beach Garden** and the **Szechwan Mahal** (Indian/Chinese), as well as restaurants in hotels. **Hilltop Hotel** restaurant probably best in Kigoma.

TOURS AND EXCURSIONS

Rubondo Island NP is reached from Mwanza by chartered aircraft. Gombe Stream NP can be reached by boat from Kigoma, as can Mahale Mountains NP (but Mahale, via the lake, is a full safari). From Mwanza you can visit the Serengeti NP via its western gate (or by chartered flights). Visits can be arranged from Mwanza to Sukuma Museum, to see cultural artifacts and Sukuma snake dancing.

USEFUL CONTACTS

Mwanza code: (0)28
Mwanza airport: (0)28 256 0067; **Tanzanian NP:** www.habari.co.tz/tanapa
Flying Doctor: (0)27 250 2830.

LAKE VICTORIA	J	F	M	A	M	J	J	A	S	O	N	D
AVERAGE TEMP. °F	70	70	70	70	70	70	68	70	70	70	70	70
AVERAGE TEMP. °C	21	21	21	21	21	21	21	21	21	21	21	21
RAINFALL in	6	7	10	15	13	3	2	3	4	5	7	8
RAINFALL mm	151	168	250	370	320	85	49	76	104	138	185	193
DAYS OF RAINFALL	13	13	18	22	18	7	5	8	11	15	18	16

6
The South

Formerly known as 'The Hell Run', the **Tanzam Highway** from Dar es Salaam to Zambia passes through some of the most beautiful scenery in Tanzania. The road is now quite good, and the journey along it much less harrowing.

By-passing the lovely **Uluguru Mountains** and the little town of **Morogoro**, the highway passes through **Mikumi National Park**, and to the north of the huge **Selous Game Reserve**, and the scenic **Udzungwa Mountains National Park**, before winding into the **Rubeho Mountains** and crossing the central plateau. The road skirts the steep ridge on which the southern highland town of **Iringa** is perched, and from where yet another magnificent game park, **Ruaha**, is easily reached. The road then rolls on towards **Mbeya** and the Zambian border.

Other than those travelling to or from Malawi and Zambia, few tourists travel down this highway, and yet much of the country through which it passes or to its south and north, embraces some of the world's finest wildlife sanctuaries, and some of its lovliest landscapes.

THE MOROGORO REGION

The country between Dar es Salaam and Morogoro is unremarkable for the first 160km (100 miles). At about this point the **Uluguru Mountains** become visible, lending grandeur to an already improving landscape. The mountains, rising to 2646m (8679ft), form part of the Eastern Arc, a broken series of ancient crystalline ranges which

CLIMATE

Generally the area follows the typical climatic patterns of the East African plateau. Days are hot while nights and mornings can be pleasantly cool (especially during the dry season). The greatest threat to travel in the southern game sanctuaries is continual heavy rain. This is most likely from mid-March to mid-May, and to a lesser extent from mid-October to December. At these times certain tracks become impassable and certain airstrips inaccessible.

Opposite: *The Ruaha River and Ruaha National Park, near Msembe.*

Right: *A baobab at sunset by the Ruaha River, home to crocodile, hippo and many water birds.*

DON'T MISS

*** Selous Game Reserve: great variety of game (including wild dogs) and bird life.
*** Ruaha National Park: another huge and beautiful wilderness with many big game species and birds.
** Mikumi National Park: only four-and-a-half hours' drive from Dar es Salaam. Lion, elephant, wild dog and leopard.
** Mufundi Area: tea estates, golf course, lovely climate and scenery, nearby Highland Lodge, superbly situated and offering horse riding, fishing, etc.
** Udzungwa National Park: beautiful montane forests rich in endemic species, fine scenery.

curves up from south-central Tanzania, reaching almost to Kilimanjaro. On the ridges are the attractive hamlets of the Luguru people, small clusters of thatched huts often perched at the very end of the high spurs.

Morogoro *

Beneath the northerly slopes of the Ulugurus snuggles the town of Morogoro. Its attractiveness owes much to the mountains, as the charm it had in German times and for some time afterwards has largely gone to seed. However, it has a lively **market**, a pleasant little rock garden and an increasing number of reasonable hotels. Morogoro also

The Morogoro Region

boasts a very testing nine-hole golf course located by the newly renovated Morogoro Hotel, which acts as the 19th hole. And there are signs of an economic upturn in the town's fortunes. There is a flourishing **agricultural college** just outside the town, and a variety of vegetables are grown on the nearby farms. Much of this produce goes to market in Dar es Salaam. Wheat, millet, sugar cane and tobacco are among the area's other crops, as well as sisal.

The town was the scene of fierce fighting during World War I, when the German forces, attacked by the British, put up stern resistance before beating a strategic retreat through the Ulugurus.

Mikumi National Park ★★

About 80km (50 miles) southwest of Morogoro, the highway bisects Mikumi National Park. It is the fourth largest national park in Tanzania, a fact which surprises many visitors, as the area they frequent is relatively small, encompassing the flood plains of the unimposing but important **Mkata River**, which flows through the park from south to north.

Surrounded on three sides by attractive mountains and hills, the park has a quiet but compelling beauty. During and just after the rains the flood plain can be as green as an Irish meadow, though the autumnal colours of the miombo woodland seen towards the end of the

---

MONEY GROWING ON TREES

• **Sisal** is a species of agave, introduced to the old German East Africa from Mexico. Hairy white string, rope and mats are made from the fibrous leaves, and at one time the industry was a money-spinner. These days labour-intensive plantations and the use of synthetic fibres have reduced demand.
• Handicrafts displayed on the stumps of trees alongside the main road at the village of Mangae, between Morogoro and Mikumi National Park, are woven by women from the fronds of the young *hyphaene palm*. Anyone purchasing mats or baskets is indirectly helping Mikumi, as the villagers begin to see the value, to themselves as well as their country, of tourism.

Below: *The rustic simplicity of Mikumi Wildlife Lodge, in the underrated Mikumi National Park.*

dry season on the slopes of the hills are deceptive – the leaves are not dying but coming to life, in anticipation of the rains.

The variety of the vegetation is matched by the diversity of animals. Mikumi has many elephants (mostly small, as elephants go), and wild dog and elusive leopard are regularly seen (though far from guaranteed). Lion are commonly encountered, as are giraffe, buffalo, zebra, buck, hippo and warthog. Birdlife is abundant.

The light is often superb, and this, together with the park's natural beauty, make it a wonderful venue for photographers. Sadly, many animals are killed on the main Tanzania–Zambia highway that bisects the park, though the road can offer some unusual photo opportunities.

Udzungwa Mountains National Park *

The Tanzam highway leaves the western boundary of Mikumi by Mikumi Village. From here, a two-hour drive to the south takes travellers alongside the picturesque Udzungwa mountains and to the entrance of the equally picturesque national park of the same name. Gazetted in 1992, the sanctuary enjoys a growing reputation due to its rare endemic plants and animals. Game viewing and bird watching can be enormously rewarding, but neither are easy and visitors should be prepared for some stiff walking and scrambling. Among recent exciting discoveries are the Sanje crested mangabey (a monkey) and a previously unknown francolin, very similar to the hill partridge of the Chinese Himalaya. Despite its rare animal and plant life, Udzungwa's most popular attraction is the Sanje waterfall, from the top of which hikers are treated to glorious views

Below: *A noisy redbilled hornbill, commonly found across the southern region.*

across the northern Kilombero Valley and the Selous. Reasonable accommodation is available in Sanje Village and near the park headquarters. There are three camp sites within the park.

The Ruaha Gorge *

Beyond Mikumi village the Tanzam highway climbs up through the Rubeho Mountains, before descending to follow the course of the Ruaha River, affording, at one point, fine views down the Ruaha Gorge.

The gorge's rock-strewn river is commanded by steep slopes to the south and more gradual slopes to the north, covered by **baobabs**. In the dry season, in sharp light, their bulbous trunks and angular filigree of brances shine silver-white, enhancing the baobab's reputation, among many Africans, as being inhabited by ghosts. There is a pleasant camp site in this 'Baobab Valley', alongside the river.

IRINGA

Beyond this world of spirits lies the plateau country around Iringa, capital of the Southern Highlands. Its situation atop a steep-sided ridge was strategic, as the Germans (who were largely responsible for the town's development) were well aware.

The people of the area, the **Hehe**, helped to stem the southerly expansion of the Maasai in the 19th century, and in 1889, under their formidable chief **Mkwawa**, ambushed a German-led military column as it approached from Morogoro. Using spears and other simple weapons the Hehe slaughtered almost half the German contingent, capturing guns and ammunition. Five years later Mkwawa's unfinished fort at Kalenga, 32km (20 miles) down the Ruaha track from Iringa, was attacked and the Hehe routed.

Iringa's grisly history is implicit in the names of two hills which overlook the town. One, Lundamatwe, means 'Collection of Skulls', the other, Tagamenda, 'Throw Cloths'. The slopes of the former were once festooned with the severed heads of enemy warriors, those of the latter with the clothes of the Hehe dead.

DEATH OF MKWAWA, CHIEF OF THE HEHE

Chief Mkwawa was a renowned soldier, and it is believed that the name of his tribe came from his battle cry, a blood-curdling 'hee-hee'. After the German-led attack upon his fort at Kalenga in 1894, he fled, fighting a guerilla warfare from the hills. The Germans put a price on his head but it was only four years later, in 1898, that the same head was shattered by a bullet. Mkwawa, cornered, shot himself rather than face the inevitable hangman. His opponents, for reasons best known to themselves, had the head hacked off and shipped to Germany. In 1954 the much-travelled skull returned to Kalenga, courtesy of the German government, and is now on display in the small museum there.

The Germans were forced out by the British during World War I, but Iringa retains the air of a dilapidated Bavarian market town. Traces of its old beauty are still apparent, with its lovely jacarandas, its avenues of eucalyptus and pine, and the occasional show of exotic flowers. It even has a Railway Hotel, a rather odd thing to find at the top of a 200 foot-high escarpment and 80km (50 miles) from the nearest railway.

Isimila ★

About 23km (14 miles) west of Iringa is one of the most important archeological sites in Africa, Isimila. Stone tools, such as hand-axes, cleavers and hammers, used some 60,000 years ago by people of the Acheulean Age, have been found in abundance, together with the bones of elephants, antelopes and pigs. Some of the bones bear the slash-marks of butchery, and some belonged to creatures now extinct, including ancient evolutionary offshoots of the giraffe and hippo lines (the ancient hippo, *gorgops*, had eyes on stalks, a little like a crab). Not far from the site are some arresting rock stacks rising to a height of 15m (50ft).

Ruaha National Park ★★★

Ruaha is one of the premier wildlife parks in Africa, and, with an area of 13,000 km² (5000 sq miles), is only slightly smaller than the Serengeti. The park's headquarters, at **Msembe,** is 130km (80 miles) west of Iringa, along a good dirt track, which passes a series of Hehe villages.

Opposite: *Tea pickers performing their highly selective task on the estates at Mufindi in the attractive Southern Highlands.*
Right: *Stone Age tools from the important site at Isimila, near Iringa.*

The famous East African ornithologist John Williams once said of Ruaha that 'of all the East African faunal preserves it is the park of the future'. More than a quarter of a century later his prophecy is beginning to come true, as this glorious wilderness becomes better known and developed.

The **Ruaha River** and its tributaries (some of them 'sand rivers' for the greater part of the year) are the focal points for most visitors, as they are for many animals. Along these watercourses grow wild figs, tamarinds, palms and the lovely winterthorn trees *Faidherbia albida*, all of which provide food and shade for the animals, and which give greener definition to the often dry, always magnificent landscapes.

Parts of the land are dominated by baobabs, though in general the country is covered by *Combretum* and *Commiphora* woodland, with a scattering of acacia. Here and there are open areas of black-cotton grassland, where ostriches, Grant's gazelle and sometimes lion and cheetah might be found.

Ruaha is usually open throughout the year, and is wonderfully green during and just after the rains.

Mufindi Tea Estates ★★

A wonderful complement to a safari in Ruaha is a visit to Mufindi, which is about 100km (60 miles) southwest of Iringa. After the rigours of the bush, the relative comforts

---

RUAHA SAFARI

Some of the highlights are:
• **Elephant:** Ruaha is renowned for its huge bull elephants, now recovering after the poaching atrocities of the 1980s. Family groups are often seen bathing or crossing the river at suitable places, such as Msembe. Calves will hang onto their mother's tail with their trunks as they step into the water, or, if completely submerged, will use their trunks as periscopes.
• **Roan antelope:** present in certain areas although not always seen.
• **Greater kudu:** quite common in many parts of the park.
• **Crocodile** and **hippo:** found in various reaches of the river, including the so-called 'Hippo Pool' close to the bridge which takes visitors into the park.
• **Birdlife:** seen throughout the Park, though the river drive is one of the best areas. Species include the rare Eleanora's falcon (a passage migrant) and Ruaha red-billed hornbill.

BOEHM'S BEE-EATER

Eight members of the beautiful bee-eater family might be seen in The Selous. One of them, Boehm's Bee-eater, is quite uncommon, but might be easily observed and photographed in the Rufiji River Camp, where it nests. The nest is little more than a tunnel in the ground, sometimes astonishingly close to a well-used footpath. Patrons of the camp can be quite alarmed when a slender, bottle-green missile comes hurtling from its underground 'silo' to perch on a nearby branch, awaiting the next unfortunate bee (which the birds devenom by holding them in their bill and rubbing them against a branch).

and cool climate of the highlands are a rest cure for body and soul.

The tea estates at Mufindi are interesting, with a pleasing geometric beauty. Guided tours around the processing factory can be arranged, but it is the adjacent golf course, a soothing green after the scorched fairways at the coast, and the forest and fishing lakes, which attract most visitors. The nearby Fox's Higland Lodge provides a welcoming and wonderful base.

SELOUS GAME RESERVE

The Selous (pronounced 'Sell-oo') is the oldest and biggest game reserve in Africa and among one of the wildest sanctuaries on earth. The reserve extends over more than 50,000km² (19,300 sq miles) of miombo woodland, terminalia thicket, open grassland and gallery forest, watered by the **Rufiji River**, its network of tributaries, and its ox-bow lakes. Very few travellers venture into the almost trackless wastes south of the Rufiji, and those who do must be entirely self-sufficient. The reserve's northern sector is the only area in any way developed for tourism, but even this is huge and wild,

Opposite: *Boat safari helmsmen and game scouts on Lake Tagala in Selous Game Reserve.*
Right: *The Rufiji River, which waters the huge wilderness of the Selous Game Reserve.*

although its vast topography is given scale by hills, the adjacent Uluguru mountains, as well as the Rufiji itself.

Northern Selous: Eastern Sector

The drive to the Selous from Dar es Salaam, southwards along about 130km (80 miles) of recently laid tarmac to Kibiti, and 105km (66 miles) of dirt track beyond that passes, in its latter stages, through a series of simple villages. A simple camp (**Mbega**) is situated just outside the Reserve's gate at Mtemere, and a little way beyond the gate a more popular, much older camp, **Rufiji River**.

The river from which it takes its name captures the imagination, and a boat safari, through pods of wallowing hippo and past basking crocodiles, is the highlight of the visit for most people. Buffalo, waterbuck, and impala can usually be seen in the water meadows. Giraffes have not yet found their way across the Rufiji, but might be seen on the northern banks, while elephant and lion are always possibilities. Water birds are plentiful, and include the African skimmer, kingfishers, goliath heron and the nocturnal Pel's fishing owl.

In some places the river banks are lined by avenues of headless borassus palms, their spindle-shaped boles like regiments of giant aliens. Against a Selous sunset, the river glittering with fragmented light and the Uluguru Mountains blue-grey in the distance, the palms make a fantastic sight.

RUGBY MEN

It was an English ex-public schoolboy by the name of **Ionides** who was responsible for expanding the Selous to its present vastness. Nellie Grant, mother of the writer Elspeth Huxley, met him in 1959 and reported that 'he is a bit round the bend' (he was known to scorn underclothes, allow himself to be bitten by venomous snakes and eat hornbills). He is buried at the foot of Nandanga Mountain. Also buried in the reserve, and also a product of Rugby School in England, was **Frederick Courtney Selous**, a white hunter for Theodore Roosevelt and a leader of the famous scouts who were sent by Cecil Rhodes to capture land in what became Rhodesia (now Zimbabwe). Selous was also slightly eccentric, with the habit of hunting lions from horseback minus his trousers; his grave is close to the spot, near the Beho-Beho river, where he was shot by a sniper's bullets in the midst of a skirmish during World War I.

From their bare tops, here and there along the river, fish eagles throw back their snow-white heads and send their evocative call echoing along the waterway.

The bush around the Rufiji River Camp is almost as interesting, with mature miombo woodland close by, reminding northern visitors of the broad-leaved woodlands of home, and less familiar tracts of whistling thorn beyond. Wild dogs, elephants and other animals might sometimes be seen in the shady miombo woodland, with giraffes, greater kudu, eland, zebra and wildebeest often among the whistling thorn. In the dry season they file through the acacias to drink at the river, or the attractive little Lake Mzizima, a short drive from the camp.

Northern Selous: East-Central Sector

A leisurely one-and-a-half hour's drive or so from Rufiji River brings the traveller to the centre of a delightful area of *Terminalia spinosa* parkland and waterside terraces which, after the rains, are beautifully lush and green. Plentiful water and grazing attract a variety of game, and lions are common, though (as always in the southern parks) the wildlife enthusiast or photographer has to work hard for his or her rewards. **Selous Safari**, **Impala**, **Mbuyu** and **Manze** Camps, all on the Rufiji or adjacent lakes, serve this area.

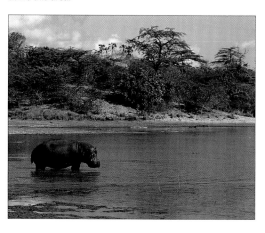

Right: *One of the Rufiji River's many hippos takes to the water after a night's grazing on the banks.*

Left: Endangered because of their susceptibility to diseases borne by domesticated canines, sightings of wild dog have become a highlight of safaris in the southern national parks.

Northern Selous: Beho-Beho Sector

West of the Mbuyu area the *Terminalia* woodland degenerates into scrub as the land rises towards Beho-Beho, an expanse of hilly terrain and open grassland which Dr Alan Rodgers, one of the greatest authorities on the Selous, has described as 'some of the most magnificent wildlife country in East Africa'. Many game animals, including lion, wild dogs and hyenas, seem to agree with him. Elephant are often seen in the groves of doum palm alongside watercourses or sand rivers, and sable antelope inhabit the wooded hills in the northwest.

Rhino, once common in the area, are beginning to recover from the poaching blitz of the 1980s, and hippo and crocodiles may be seen in one of Beho-Beho's main features, **Lake Tagalala**. Ospreys, palm-nut vultures and many species of water or grassland birds might be observed in the vicinity of the lake.

Other attractions in the **Beho-Beho sector** include the **hot springs**, a pretty picnic spot where you may bathe or swim in the warm waters, **Stiegler's Gorge** (on the Rufiji) and **Selous' grave**, close to Beho-Beho Camp. Among the old trenches overlooking the spot where Selous met his death, rifle cartridges may still be discovered. Visitors to the reserve still sometimes place

FOOT SAFARIS

In the Selous, as in other game reserves (but **not** most National Parks), visitors can experience some of the thrills of old-time safaris by walking, rather than driving, through the bush, accompanied by an armed game scout. Such safaris can be disappointing for photographers of big game, as animals will usually avoid people on foot and vanish into the vegetation. Now and again, however, lions, elephants or buffalo remain unaware of approaching humans, allowing for an exciting, though rarely dangerous, encounter. Big game or not, a foot safari allows participants a fascinating insight into life in the bush, where the spoor of a jackal, the glimpse of a wild flower, the smell of a dead antelope, or the sound of a snapping twig can arouse a whole spectrum of emotions, including wonder – and fear.

SACRED SCARABS

There are various species of
scarab beetle, or as they are
more prosaically known, dung
beetles. The scarab was sacred
to the ancient Egyptians, who
perhaps recognized its enterprise and industry. During or
immediately after the rains, the
beetles can often be seen pad-
dling balls of buffalo or elephant dung across the tracks,
using their back pair of legs.
The female beetle, after burying
the ball of dung in a suitable
spot, lays her eggs in it. The
resulting grub enters the world
surrounded by what (to them)
is an irresistible and seemingly
inexhaustible supply of food.

Above right: *Hot springs
in the Beho-Beho area of
the northern Selous.*
Below: *Sand Rivers
Lodge, overlooking the
Rufiji River, Selous
Game Reserve.*

wild flowers on the grave in sentimental but sincere tribute, using beer bottles as vases (Selous, who was teetotal,
might not have approved).

Beho-Beho and its adjacent countryside encompasses
a first-class luxury lodge, **Sand Rivers**, which is on the
Rufiji River, as well as the long-established **Beho-Beho
Camp**, situated on the slopes of a hill above a small tribu-
tary of the Beho-Beho river. A third camp, **Sable
Mountain Lodge**, now stands just outside the Beho-Beho
area (and the reserve) close to the Matambwe Gate.

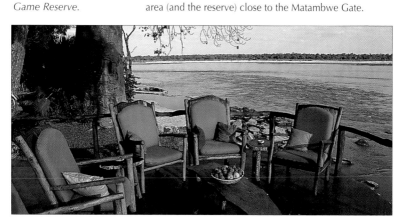

The South at a Glance

Mid-May to mid-October dry, mornings and evenings cool. Rains usually fall mid-October to mid-May, peaking Mar–Apr. Rains can restrict travel on certain tracks within parks.

Most visitors fly into Dar on scheduled international or locally chartered flights.

Visitors usually travel by charter flights or safari company vehicles. Long-distance buses and taxis are available in towns.

Morogoro
Hotel Oasis, tel: (Mor) (023) 261 3010/260 3535, mobile: 0744 377601/602, hoteloasis@morogoro.net
Morogoro Hotel, tel: (Mor) (023) 261 3270. As Oasis.

Iringa
Old Farmhouse, kisolanza@cats-net.com Kisolanza, 50km (30 miles) from Iringa.
Fox's Highland Lodge, central reservations tel: (0)22 286 357, cell: (0)713 237 422/(0)754 237 422/(0)784 237 422.

Mbeya
Utengule Country Hotel, tel: (0)25 256 0100. Most attractive of the fairly limited options.
Mt Livingstone Hotel, tel: (0)25 250 3331-4, cell: 0741 350 480. Modest but clean and comfortable and probably best of town centre options.

Mikumi NP
Fox's Safari Camp, central reservations tel: (0)22 286 357, cell: (0)713 237 422/(0)754 237 422/(0)784 237 422.
Fox's Vuma Hills, central reservations tel: (0)22 286 357, cell: (0)713 237 422/(0)754 237 422/(0)784 237 422.
Mikumi Wildlife Camp, tel: (0)22 260 0470.

Ruaha NP
Jungomero Tented Camp, tel: (0)22 212 8485, cell: 0748 953 551.
Mwagusi Sand River Camp, tel: (UK) 020 8846 9363.
Ruaha River Lodge, tel: (0)23 244 0194, cell: (0)811 327 706. Long-established, popular.

Selous Game Reserve
Sand Rivers Luxury Lodge, no direct bookings, but Nomad's (the owning group) tel: (0)27 255 3819.
Selous Safari Camp, tel: (0)22 212 8485. On bank of Rufiji, by Lake Siwando.
Selous Wildlife Lodge, central reservations (0)22 260 2888, marketing@malalaluxury lodges.com On Simbazi River.
Rufiji River Camp, (0)22 212 866/3. Popular camp on tree-shaded cliffs by Rufiji River.
Beho-Beho Camp, tel: (0)22 260 0352-4. Set among hills by attractive, open country.
Lake Manze Camp, tel: (0)22 245 2005/6, reservations@adventurecamps.co.tz www.adventurecamps.co.tz Tents (en-suite bathrooms).
Mivumo River Lodge, central

reservations (0)22 260 2888, marketing@malalaluxury lodges.com New luxury lodge close to Steigler's Gorge.
The Retreat, central reservations +41 79 444 03 28, retreat@bluewin.ch www.retreatsafaris.co.tz Luxurious; in far northwest of Reserve.

Udzungwa NP
Udzungwa Mountain View, tel: (0)23 262 0466. Simple; 10 minutes' walk from Mang'ula.
Twiga Hotel, simple hotel in Mang'ula.

Most visitors eat in the lodges, hotels, etc.

Morogoro
Walks in Uluguru Mountains, birding, nine-hole golf course.

Iringa Area
Mkwawa Museum, Kalenga. Dedicated to Hehe chief.
Mufindi Tea Estates & golf course (150km southwest). Good birding, but a 1–2 night stay is better than brief visit. Closer to Iringa is the **Isimila Stone Age site**, worth seeing.

Mbeya
There are many walks around Mbeya. Ask at your hotel.

Tanzanian NP: www.habari. co.tz/tanapa **Selous:** www.tanzania-web.com/ parks/selous.htm **Flying Doctor:** tel: (0)27 250 2830.

7
Zanzibar, Pemba and Mafia

Forty kilometres (25 miles) east of Bagamoyo, off the mid-Tanzanian coast, lies the island of Unguja or, as it is more commonly known to westerners, Zanzibar. It is only 85km (53 miles) long and 20km (12 miles) wide, but for centuries its importance has been out of all proportion to its size. In the 19th century it was said that 'when the flute is played in Zanzibar, they dance at the lakes', a tribute to the far-reaching powers of the Omani Sultans who made Zanzibar the seat of their Imamate, and their home. It was the earlier sultans, particularly **Said the Great**, founder of the Zanzibar sultanate in 1832, who brought prosperity to the islands, largely by encouraging the planting of cloves, and by promoting the slave trade on which the plantations depended.

But there is much more to Unguja, and its sister island **Pemba**, away to the north, than history. They are low-lying, with no significant mountains or rivers, but they are pleasant, fertile places, their sultry air still heavy, at times, with the scent of spices.

A BRIEF HISTORY OF ZANZIBAR

The early history of the islands remains obscure, although they were mentioned in *The Periplus of the Erythrean Sea*, a seafarers' guide written by a **Greek** merchant in AD 60. It is fairly certain that **Arabs** had begun to settle in Zanzibar by the 9th century, and that 400 years later **Shirazi Persians** made their home there. By 1045 the indigenous population had already adopted Islam. Zanzibar's first

CLIMATE

The climate of Zanzibar, Pemba and Mafia is typically coastal: generally hot and humid but often tempered by sea breezes. Average daytime temperatures are around 30°C (86°F). The hottest months are from November to March, but from June to October the southeast monsoon brings cooler, drier weather. From March to May the Long Rains bring some heavy showers. The Short Rains (less predictable and lighter) occur between October and December.

Opposite: *The old Arab fort and House of Wonders (behind) in Stone Town.*

DON'T MISS

*** **Stone Town:** a leisurely stroll around the old streets is what Zanzibar is all about.
** **Beaches:** on the northeast coast, the finest in Tanzania.
** **Spice Tours:** a great way to take in the full breadth of Zanzibar island and its history up-country.
** **Pemba Island:** interesting ruins; remote way of life; good fishing, diving and snorkelling.
* **Mafia Island:** not often visited, but good for fishing, diving and snorkelling. Site of Tanzania's first marine park.

Opposite: *The crumbling house of Tippu Tip, best known of Zanzibar's slave traders and a prosperous merchant.*
Below: *Graves at Zanzibar's first mosque, the 12th-century house of worship at Kizimkazi.*

mosque, at Kizimkazi, was built in 1107. The Persians and Arabs passed on commercial know-how as well as genes, inspiring vigorous trade with countries as far afield as China. This buoyant interchange was depressed by two centuries of **Portuguese** rule, beginning in 1500. But by 1700 the Portuguese were in retreat, ousted by the resurgent **Omani Arabs**.

Omani rule along the coast soon became absolute, though there were many feuds among the powerful families, and a few indigenous chiefs retained power in the

Zanzibar Island (Unguja)

remoter areas. But Zanzibar's rise to fame – and notoriety – really began in 1832, when **Sultan Seyid Said** (Said the Great), chose to control his extensive Imamate from Zanzibar rather than Muscat, the Omani capital on the Arabian peninsula

Capital of the Slave Trade

On the death of Said in 1856, the Omani sultanate broke away from Zanzibar. By then Zanzibar and Pemba were well on the way to prosperity, based on the dramatic expansion of the **clove** plantations, and the equally dramatic expansion of the **slave trade**.

The slave trade had existed for centuries before the sultans came to Zanzibar, but not on such a terrible and escalating scale. The British, who had established an early presence in Zanzibar, opposed the trade and, through their political agents, notably **Atkins Hamerton** and **John Kirk**, gained the confidence of the two most influential sultans of the period, Said and his son **Barghash**. The British were instrumental in limiting and finally ending the slave trade, though it was almost 50 years after the closing of the infamous Zanzibar slave market, in 1873, that slavery was completely eradicated from mainland Tanganyika.

TIPPU TIP

The best known of all Zanzibari slave traders was Tippu Tip (his real name was Hamed Bin Muhammed El Murjebi). He was ruthless and determined, but also a man of intelligence, ability and courage. On one occasion, when hit by three arrows during a skirmish, he turned on his assailants and, together with his companions, killed more than 1000 within an hour. Stanley regarded him as 'the most remarkable man I had met among the Arabs, Waswahili and the half-castes in Africa', and the slaver, with a personal retinue of 96 (including his 35 wives and concubines) sailed from Zanzibar to West Africa as part of Stanley's final expedition in 1887. Tippu Tip enjoyed retirement as a wealthy and respected gentleman, in his house in Zanzibar Town. The house still stands.

**BRITAIN'S MAN
IN ZANZIBAR**

John Kirk was, perhaps, the best-known of several very able British consuls attached to Zanzibar. A former travelling partner of Livingstone's and a friend and advisor of Sultan Barghash, his influence was enormous. He helped to end the slave trade, and also assisted various explorers (although Stanley detested him). His house at Mbweni, just south of Zanzibar town, and built for him by Barghash, may still be visited. It was here that Kirk, an expert botanist, lovingly created an experimental garden, introducing improved varieties of native food-plants and trees, and other plants likely to prove of economical value to the islands.

The Explorers

From the late 1850s to the mid-1870s, up to 30,000 slaves a year were brought to Zanzibar. Throughout the same period, a series of extraordinary men were heading in the opposite direction. **Burton** and **Speke** passed through Zanzibar in 1857, to seek the source of the Nile which Speke discovered on his second attempt in 1862, accompanied by Grant. In 1866 **Livingstone** set out from Zanzibar on his last journey, returning (in a coffin) in 1874. In 1872 **H.M. Stanley** sailed into Zanzibar to a hero's welcome after his historic meeting with Livingstone in Ujiji.

The explorers were often helped by the Zanzibari slave traders, who, however ruthless, regarded slaving as legitimate business. The sultans, too, would have been puzzled by western moralities, not least because of American and European involvement in the West African slave trade. They signed anti-slavery legislation only under pressure, but the benefits which the sultans brought to Zanzibar should not be overlooked. Their legacy included a thriving economy, which the clove plantations easily sustained long after the decline of the slave trade, telegraph and shipping links with Europe, and in Zanzibar Town a clean water supply.

Revolution

Zanzibar became a British protectorate in 1890, and for more than 70 years enjoyed relative peace and prosperity. Apart from a brief naval action at the start of World War I, when the German battle cruiser *Koenigsberg* shelled and sank the British warship *Pegasus* in Zanzibar harbour, the islands were not directly affected by the two world wars. As soon as the British left, however, *Pax Britannica* left on the same tide. In 1963 **Sayyid Jamshid Bin Abdulla Bin Khalif**, last of the Zanzibari sultans, came to the throne. In January 1964, one month after Zanzibar's independence, he was overthrown in a bloody revolution. About 13,000 people, mostly Arabs, were slaughtered in an orgy of killing. A generation later, peace (if not political stability) has returned to the islands, which are beginning to recover some of their former autonomy and prosperity, and to attract more tourists.

Above: *The gazebo in Jamituri Gardens on Stone Town's seafront.*
Opposite: *'Livingstone's House', Zanzibar. The house was, in fact, made available to the explorer by Sultan Barghash.*

THE STONE TOWN

The Stone Town is Zanzibar's old quarter. It has been called 'the only functioning historical city in East Africa' and is so little changed since the 1850s (at least structurally), that Burton and Speke, it seems, might just have left for the interior. The best way to appreciate this is to walk, as the explorers did, through the old streets.

Seafront

There are no prescribed routes for a tour of Stone Town – but perhaps the seafront is an appropriate place to start. People arriving by sea will pass the old dhow harbour as they leave the dockside complex. The great ocean-going dhows are mostly gone, but visitors should see smaller *jahazi* or *mashua*, still common and basically unchanged throughout the years. At sea, lateen sails silhouetted against a flaming sunset, their romantic appeal can still be captivating. Smaller dhows are still common.

**DOORWAYS TO
HISTORY**

Zanzibar doors have become
renowned. Custom ordained
that the doorway of a house
should be built before the
house itself, presumably to
exert a benign influence over
the completed building. The
ritual was given added
strength by Koranic scripts
and representational carvings
which adorn the doorways.
The Zanzibar door was traditionally made of teak, and was
set in a square frame, covered
by delicate and slender
carvings. Indian influences
during the 19th century
modified this prototype, producing doors with arched tops
and more elaborate floral
designs. Motifs to be seen on
such doors include the lotus
(symbol of reproductive
power), the fish (fertility),
the chain (security) and the
frankincense tree (wealth).

A short distance from the dockyard gate Mizingani
Road begins its southwesterly course along one of the
most historic seafronts in the world. Near its northern end
is the ornately attractive **Ismaili Dispensary**, (now a cultural centre) presented to the Aga Khan's followers in
Zanzibar on the occasion of Queen Victoria's Jubilee. A
little further along the road, still heading southwest, is the
former Sultan's Palace, now the **People's Palace**, and
open to the public. First occupied by a reigning sovereign
in 1911, it previously accommodated members of the
royal family and harem. In the graveyard alongside, Said
the Great and sultans lie buried. The interior of the
palace is comfortably rather than splendidly furnished,
but it provides interesting insights into a vanished and
exotic period of Zanzibar's history.

Adjacent to the palace is the **House of Wonders**, the
Beit el-Ajaib, built by Sultan Barghash in 1883. Together
with the original palace it was damaged by shell-fire
during a scuffle for the accession in 1896, when British
warships intervened, precipitating 'the shortest war in
history' (it lasted for 45 minutes). The Beit el-Ajaib has
now become a museum, minus the lions and the other
animals which were once kept caged outside its gates. It
contains the most beautiful examples of 'Zanzibar doors'
in East Africa.

Right: *The House of
Wonders, built as a
ceremonial palace in
1883 by Sultan Barghash.*

A little further down the seafront stands the **Arab Fort**, with its ochre-coloured walls. Never more than a primitive structure, it withstood an attack by the Mazrui Arabs from Mombasa in 1754, and was afterwards used as a gaol. As late as 1890 criminals sentenced to death were still publicly beheaded by the sword, just outside the walls at the back of the fort. Enclosed by a promontory to the west of the fort is the district known as Shangani, 'The Place of Beads'. The original **slave market** (in the square now overlooked by the Serena Hotel) once stood here and, appropriately, the house of **Tippu Tip**, most notorious of the Zanzibar slavers, can be found nearby, in a shadowy, seldom-visited corner of the town.

A few doors away is the **Africa House Hotel**, a less ominous building with its own nostalgia. Formerly the British Club, it clings, with stiff upper lip, to its colonial past. Its seaward-facing terrace is popular at sundown. The **Zanzibar Hotel**, in the same district, is another interesting old building, its rooms traditionally constructed from mangrove poles. The poles, impervious to termites, are still used throughout East Africa, and their export to the Gulf and elsewhere, by dhow, is one of the oldest forms of trade in the region.

In the southern area of Stone Town is the **National Museum** now virtually derelict within. At the back of the museum is the oldest carved door in Stone Town. Close by on Kaunda Road are the **High Courts**, with their blend of Arabic and Portuguese architecture, and the **State House** designed by the British architect John Sinclair, whose love of the Islamic style contributed much to Stone Town.

Zanzibar (Stone Town)

HOTEL INDEX
1. AFRICA HOUSE
2. BWAWANI
3. DHOW PALACE; BAGHANI HOUSE
4. 236 HURUMZI
5. TEMBO HOUSE
6. ZANZIBAR
7. ZANZIBAR SERENA
8. COCO DE MER
9. KARIBU INN
10. INTERNATIONAL
11. CHAVDA
12. VICTORIA HOUSE
13. MAZSON'S

FINDING YOUR WAY IN STONE TOWN

• **Walking** is undoubtedly the best (and often only) way to negotiate the fascinating narrow streets of Stone Town.

• **Guides** are not essential, but the best of them, often older, know their town and its absorbing history. Visitors should ask for a guide at their hotel or any tourist centre.

• If you choose to discover Stone Town on your own, however, you can 'lose' yourself in the maze of alleyways without too much fear of being lost for long, or of having anything **stolen**, though visitors should use a little common sense (e.g. by not wearing expensive jewellery).

• Don't take **photographs** without asking.

• Please respect Islamic modesty by wearing clothes that are not too revealing.

THE CATHEDRAL

Stone Town's Cathedral Church of Christ, built on the site of the old slave market, is an imposing building. Inside the altar was erected on the same spot as the slave whipping post had been, and a stained-glass window commemorates the British sailors who died on anti-slaving patrols. On a pillar beside the chancel is a crucifix, made from the tree under which Livingstone's heart was buried. Interred behind the cathedral altar are the remains of Bishop Steere, who supervised the building of the cathedral and who, every Friday, had the Victorian cheek to preach to Muslims in the adjoining Chapel of the Blessed Sacrament. This obviously didn't upset the reigning sultan, Barghash, who donated a clock to adorn the Cathedral tower.

Markets Old and Young

Zanzibar's seafront reeks of history, but the true adventure of Stone Town is to lose yourself in its maze of alleyways and high-walled buildings, and experience the day-to-day life of this sometimes squalid, always exciting hotchpotch. Changa Bazaar and Gizenga Street are among the most interesting. Except in the heat of the afternoon the streets bustle with unpretentious enterprise. The tiny shops are home, as well as business, to a multitude of traders and craftsmen, their goods and handiwork awaiting buyers throughout the slow-paced day. Meanwhile clocksmiths sit cross-legged on raised floors, surrounded by heaps of broken watches, tailors pedal away on sewing machines, and coffee sellers weave through the crowds with their Arabic-style pots, heated on trays of smouldering charcoal.

Close to the town's main markets, just west of Creek Road, is the **Cathedral Church of Christ** which, until 1873, was the site of the infamous slave market. Here, up to 300 slaves or more were herded and paraded each day in the late afternoon and subjected to the most intimate and embarrassing scrutiny. Muscles and teeth were examined, sticks were thrown for the male slaves to retrieve (to test their basic fitness), and the younger, more attractive women were lasciviously fondled.

Zanzibar's Roman Catholic cathedral, **St Joseph's**, on the edge of Shangani, has a less disturbing history. There are mosques too, as one might expect, the most notable being the **Aga Khan**, the

Left: *Just a few of the spices and fruits to be seen (and sampled) in Zanzibar.*
Opposite top: *Coffee is served – thick, black and strong.*
Opposite bottom: *The Cathedral Church of Christ, founded in 1873 on the slave market.*

Bohora, and the **Malindi**. Hinduism is represented by the **Shakti Temple**. Other buildings of interest include the old British Consulate, where several famous explorers stayed, the Hamamni Persian Baths and, on Kenyatta Road, General Mathews House (now a dental surgery).

Sadly many of the more traditional shops are now devoted to souvenirs, or even Internet centres, but old Zanzibar is never far away.

AROUND UNGUJA ISLAND

Zanzibar's blend of troubled history and relaxing peaceful-ness can be experienced outside, as well as inside, the Stone Town. So-called **'Spice Tours'** introduce the visitor to the fascinating world of Zanzibar's spice-growing areas, and are usually combined with a history lesson. Tourists will catch some interesting glimpses of life among the villages, with their little mud-and-wattle houses roofed with palm thatch or corrugated iron. And on the roads they might see Indian-style ox-carts or Zanzibar's unique country buses which, with their wooden coachwork, glass-less windows and slatted seats, look more like early 19th-century railway carriages, and are just about as comfortable.

After leaving town, the Spice Tours pass **Livingstone's House**. The missionary-explorer stayed here in 1866 prior to his final expedition. A little further north is **Marahubi Palace**, built by Sultan Barghash to house his harem. He did not live

---

SKELETONS – BUT NOT IN THE CUPBOARDS

The custom of burying slaves alive in the walls of houses under construction is thought to have been fairly common in old Zanzibar. Skeletons were discovered in the foundations of the old Cable and Wireless building, erected on the site of the original slave market at Shangani by Sultan Barghash to bring enlightenment to Zanzibar. A more awful irony distinguishes a building called Mambo Msigee on the tip of the Shangani promontory. It was formerly occupied by such anti-slavery luminaries as the Universities Mission to Central Africa and Sir John Kirk, who were all blithely unaware that living slaves had been entombed in the walls which sheltered them.

SPICE TOURS

The **clove** is still king on Zanzibar and Pemba, but with declining markets there has been some pressure to diversify, and people taking the Spice Tour might be shown nutmeg, black pepper, cinnamon, cardamom, chilli, vanilla, peppermint and the sharply citrus-fragrant lemon grass. Also charming the senses are an array of exotic fruits – plantains and bananas, mangos, pawpaws, breadfruit, jackfruit, avocados, guavas, mulberries, durians, litchis, pomegranates, oranges, grapefruit, and limes. Spice tours can be arranged through your hotel or a tourist information centre, but shop around and agree on an itinerary and fee before setting out.

ENDANGERED MONKEY, SCARCE LEOPARD

Jozani Forest's main attraction is the Zanzibar red colobus, *Colobus badius kirkii*, a beautiful and endangered monkey endemic to the Island and named after the well-known British Consul. Other wildlife is limited but interesting, and includes Sykes monkeys, suni antelopes, bush pigs, bush babies, hyraxes and mongooses. The Zanzibar leopard, thought until recently to be extinct, is now known to be alive and well and living (albeit precariously) in the bush and scrub of the southern part of the island.

to enjoy his visits there, and 11 years after his death it burned down. It is now in ruins, but ruins can be romantic, and Marahubi's melancholic wistfulness is not unpleasant. Further north still is another palace, **Mtoni**, once occupied by Said the Great and his huge household. Just through Bububu village are the Chuini ruins, a three level water system, supplied by an aquaduct, built to ensure constant running water in the mid 19th century, before the invention of electricity. Here you can enjoy a sundowner overlooking the Indian Ocean at Hakuna Matata Beach Lodge which is built in and around the ruins.

Less than 20km (12 miles) to the north of Mtoni is **Mangapwani**. Here, by a beautiful crescent of white sand shelving into the blue ocean, lies a dark coral cave said (probably without foundation) to have been used for holding slaves after 1873, when their export from Zanzibar was forbidden. Another place of historical interest north of Zanzibar Town are the disused **Persian Baths** at Kidichi, built by Sultan Said.

In the centre of Zanzibar Island, at **Dunga**, are the ruins of a fortified palace, former home of a tyrannical local chief. Further south, near Pete, is **Jozani Forest**, a wildlife sanctuary where endemic and endangered Zanzibar red colobus monkeys may be observed. And in the extreme south, some 30km (20 miles) beyond Jozani, travellers will find traces of an old Shirazian settlement by the seashore at **Kizimkazi**. Its mosque was the first to be built on the East African coast (in 1107). Dolphins are found off

Left: *Clear, warm waters, for so many one of the attractions of Zanzibar, at Mangapwani, north of Stone Town.*
Opposite: *Tourists stop off at Marahubi to see the atmospheric ruins of Sultan Barghash's harem.*

Kizimkazi and boats are available for visitors who wish to see these unusual mammals.

Sea and Shore

Too much history can be cloying and a convenient complement to the past is a day or two in the present, by the sea. Zanzibar's **beaches**, particularly in the north and south ('The Sunrise Coast') are often beautiful and unspoilt, locations for lotus-eating laziness. The villagers along this coast are mostly involved in fishing, though other occupations include cattle raising, mat-making, lime-burning and the making of embroidered Muslim caps.

Another possibility is to take a boat to one of Zanzibar's offshore islets. The most popular of these is commonly known as **Prison** (*Changuu*) Island. Another islet with a sombre name is **Grave** (*Chapwani*) Island. Its name relates to the cemetery there, designated by Sultan Barghash as a graveyard for British sailors killed on anti-slavery patrols, though some graves go back to the early decades of the 19th century. Despite their names, the islands are far from grim, and are known for their beaches, swimming, snorkelling and sunbathing.

PEMBA

Nearly 50km (32 miles) to the north is an island not much smaller than Unguja itself. Pemba, known to the Arabs

Right: *Drying cloves on Pemba Island, the real 'Isle of Cloves'.*

as *Al Khudra*, the Green Island, is little visited by tourists, although it is now beginning to realize its potential.

Cloves

Like Unguja, Pemba's 19th-century history was dominated by cloves and slaves. Pemba is, in fact, the true island of cloves, and although the industry is declining and prices falling, much of Pemba is still covered by clove trees, some of them a century and a half old. During the harvest season, between July and December, the oily fragrance of cloves drifts over the island in an aromatic mist. Pickers climb the trees, which can attain a height of 15m (50ft), by means of ropes or ladders, snapping off clusters of unopened buds, greenish or yellowish-red in colour. These are collected in baskets and laid out in the sun for four to seven days, until their colour deepens into the familiar dark brown, when they are graded and packed for export. They are eventually, of course, used in cooking and baking, but also in the manufacture of aromatic and medicinal oils, and in Indonesia, to flavour cigarettes.

Around the Island

The many ruins around the island bear testimony to the its older, more general past. At **Chake Chake**, Pemba's principal town, there are remains of a 13th-century Shirazi settlement, a mosque which is said to be one of the finest of its type on the coast of East Africa, and a Muslim fort (now converted into a hospital). At **Pujini**, 11km (7 miles) north of Chake Chake, there is a 14th-century fortified settlement, and at **Ras Mkumbuu**, an attractive headland on the western coast, the ruins of an Islamic settlement established in the 9th or even 8th century.

The island has various wild animals, not least among which is the Pemba puddle frog, and an endemic fruit bat, the Pemba flying fox. But wildlife enthusiasts who seek a superabundance of beautiful creatures must go down to the sea, and beneath it. And for those who prefer less demanding pastimes, Pemba has many marvellous and virtually unknown beaches.

MAFIA ISLAND *

Situated 160km (100 miles) south of Zanzibar Island, Mafia is 394km² (152 sq miles) in area. The obvious jokes are made about it, but Mafia has no connection with Sicily and it is a safe and wonderfully secluded place to visit.

It has its own interesting history, and its relatively flat topography is not unattractive, but most visitors come to Mafia because of its beaches and its excellent reputation as a centre for sea-fishing, snorkelling and diving. Tanzania's first **marine park** is now established there.

Below: *The technology of scuba diving mixes with the timelessness of an old dhow off the coast of Zanzibar.*

Zanzibar, Pemba and Mafia at a Glance

Zanzibar, Pemba and Mafia are best mid-May to mid-October. Jan–Mar can be uncomfortably hot and humid, but monsoon breezes often temper the air. Rain in Mar–Apr, and to a lesser extent Nov–Dec, can sometimes be heavy and frustrating.

Several airlines link the mainland with Zanzibar (scheduled or charter). Regular flights, scheduled or charter, also leave Dar for Mafia but check in advance as schedules sometimes change. Regular **ferries** run from the customs house jetty in Dar, opposite St Joseph's Cathedral, to Zanzibar Town. Less frequent ferries go between Zanzibar and Pemba.

In old Stone Town it is best to walk, but you might be pestered by men acting as guides. Official guides can be hired via the better hotels. Agree fees and itinerary in advance, and ensure you and the guide can communicate. **Motor scooters** and **bicycles** can be hired. **Taxis** are plentiful and cheap in Zanzibar Town. Haggling is advised and fees should be agreed before setting off. Local **buses** are often the only choice in Pemba. They are uncomfortable and sometimes crowded but the experience can be interesting.

Zanzibar Town (Stone Town)

236 Hurumzi, cell: (0)777 423 266. Formerly 'Emerson and Green's'. Home of former merchant, beautifully redesigned. In heart of Stone Town.
Africa House, Shangani, cell: (0)777 432 340. Old, historical hotel recently upgraded. Fine views of sea from terrace.
Chavda, tel: (0)24 223 2115. Pleasant hotel in Baghani, good food.
Dhow Palace, tel: (0)24 223 3008. Imaginatively converted old mansion in Baghani.
Tembo House, tel: (Zanz) (0)24 223 2069/223 3005, tembo@ zitec.org Excellent location by historic seafront. No alcohol.
Zanzibar Palace, tel: (0)24 223 2230, cell: (0)733 079 222/047 370. Recently established old town house, sensitively renovated. Kiponda area of Stone Town.

Beach Hotels
NORTHWEST/NORTH COAST
La Gemma Dell 'Est, cell: (0)777 851 234. Large luxury hotel on fine beach at Kendwa.
Nungwi Village Beach Resort, cell: (0)754 348 598. Upper mid-range, one of best resorts on this idyllic beach.
Ras Nungwi, tel: (Zanz) (0)24 223 3767/223 2512, rasnungwi@zanzibar.net Eco-sensitive resort on beautiful beach, northern tip of Zanzibar Island. One of Zanzibar's best all-round resorts.

NORTHEASTERN COAST
Bluebay Beach Resort, tel: (Zanz) (0)24 224 0240/1/2, bluebay@twiga.com Large resort on fine beach at Kiwenga.
Mapenzi Beach Resort, tel: (0)744 414 268. Beach club on fine stretch of coast.
Matemwe Bungalows, Matemwe, northeastern coast, cell: (0)777 425 788. Very good, informal resort long popular with expats.
Mnemba Island Lodge, tel: (0)24 223 3110, mnemba@ zitec.org www.ccafrica.com Exclusive lodge on superb islet just off northeastern tip of Zanzibar Island.
Neptune Pwani, central reservations tel (Mombasa): 254 41 548 5701-3. Recently completed flagship resort of Neptune Hotels on Kiwengwa shoreline.
Ocean Paradise, tel: (0)777 439 990/1/2/3.
Zamani Zanzibar Kempinski, central reservations cell: (0)744 444 477. Upper-end luxury beach hotel.

EAST COAST
Chwaka Bay, tel: (0)24 224 0289. On fine beach by Chwaka Bay marine sanctuary.
Pongwe Beach Hotel, cell: (0)777 413 973. On superb beach. Excellent seafood.
Zanzibar Safari Club, cell: (0)777 410 318/844 482. Exclusive resort at Uroa.
Zamani Zanzibar Kempinski, cell: (0)744 444 477. Superb new upmarket hotel at Kiwenga.

Zanzibar, Pemba and Mafia at a Glance

SOUTHEASTERN/SOUTH COAST
Breezes Beach Club,
central reservations (Nairobi)
tel: +254 20 272
0835/9333/8826, cell: (0)744
440 884, info@breezes-
zanzibar.com www.breezes-
zanzibar.com One of
Zanzibar's best resorts, situated
on Bwejuu Beach near
Dongwe.
Karafu, mobile: 0741 325157,
karafu-hotel@twiga.com
www.karafuhotel.com
Situated in spacious gardens
near Michamvi, winner of
World Travel award, 2006.
The Palms, phone and contact
details as in Breezes Beach
Club. Top-class resort on same
lovely beach as 'Breezes'.
Featured in BBC's Holiday
Programme.
Sultan's Palace, +254 20 712
3156/2638. Luxurious, restful.
Fine location on the beach
near Dongwe.

WEST COAST
Mbweni Ruins Hotel, tel:
(0)24 223 5478/9. Set in
superb botanical gardens by
19th-century ruins.
Chumbe Island Lodge, tel:
(0)24 223 1040, chumbe@
zitec.org www.chumbeis
land.com Award-winning
eco-lodge, marine park and
forest reserve, 14km from
Stone Town.
Fumba Beach Lodge, cell:
(0)784 425 996, (0)773 125
078. Dive centre resort at
Fumba, west coast.
Hakuna Matata Beach Lodge,
cell: (0)777 454 892. Luxury

bungalows situated on old
Chuini Palace grounds. Best
food on the island.
Mtoni Marine Centre, tel:
(0)24 225 0140. Very popular
resort just north of Stone
Town.

Pemba
Fundu Lagoon, cell: (0)747
438 668, reservations@fundu
lagoon.com Among world's
top diving locations, on
secluded Wambaa Peninsula,
west coast.
Manta Reef Lodge, cell: (0)741
320 025. Rustic, comfortable
cabins by the sea, remote
northwest tip of island, access
by light aircraft or boat.

Mafia Island
Kinasi Mafia Island Lodge, tel:
(0)24 223 8220, cell: (0)713
242 977/324 463. Stylish lodge
overlooking Chole Bay.
Mafia Island Lodge, alongside
Mafia Island Marine Park.
Pole Pole, tel: (Dar) (0)22
260 1530, contact@pole
pole.com At Kinasi by Mafia
Island Marine Park.
Chole Mjini, tree house-style
accommodation by the sea.
Turtle hatchings (Jun–Sep),
Whale sharks (Nov–Apr), PADI
Dive Centre.

WHERE TO EAT

Some independent restaurants:
Mercury's, simple, popular.
Alongside harbour, tel: (Zanz)
(0)24 223 3076,
www.queenonline.com/
fmercury.html
The Dhow Traditional
Zanzibari dhow, just off
Stone Town harbour.
Le Spice Rendezvous, simple,
popular, Indian cuisine.

TOURS AND EXCURSIONS

All can be arranged through
your hotel or a tour agency.
Spice Tours: popular trips to
the famous spice-growing
areas. Mitu's Tours, tel: 223
1020, are among the best.
Jozani Forest: rare Zanzibar
red colobus monkeys in their
natural habitat.
Boat trips: to various offshore
islets. Can be arranged through
hotels or from waterfront.
'Swimming with dolphins': an
unedifying experience but you
usually see the dolphins.

USEFUL CONTACTS

Zanzibar code: (0)24
Ministry of Tourism: 223 2562
Zanzibar Tourist Corp: 223
0467/2344; **Dr Mehta's**
Hospital: 223 0194/337190
Flying Doctor: (0)27 250 2830.

ZANZIBAR	J	F	M	A	M	J	J	A	S	O	N	D
AVERAGE TEMP. °F	81	81	81	79	79	77	75	75	77	77	79	81
AVERAGE TEMP. °C	27	27	27	26	26	25	24	24	25	25	26	27
RAINFALL in	3	3	5	15	10	2	2	2	2	3	9	6
RAINFALL mm	78	66	138	386	249	62	45	43	51	88	220	158
DAYS OF RAINFALL	7	6	12	19	14	4	5	6	6	7	14	12

Travel Tips

Tourist Information

Tanzania Tourist Board (Dar) can be contacted on tel: +255 (0)22 211 1244/1245, email: safari@ud.co.tz www.tanzania touristboard.com

Tanzania Tourist Board (Arusha), tel: (0)27 205 0025, cell: (0)754 420 258, email: culturaltourism@habari.co.tz www.tanzaniatouristboard.com

Zanzibar Tourist Corporation, tel: (0)24 223 0467/2344. There are many other websites devoted to Tanzania and its various tourist attractions.

Entry Requirements

A valid passport. Most visitors will also need an entry visa. Three-month single entry tourist visas are available at Tanzanian embassies around the world, price subject to nationality. Contact your nearest embassy or visit www. tanzaniantouristboard.com

Customs

Personal effects may be imported for the duration of your visit duty free. A customs bond may in very infrequent instances be demanded of visitors bringing in expensive filming equipment etc but most tourists will not be troubled. Firearms require a special permit.

A duty free allowance is effected on one litre of liquor, 200 cigarettes, 50 cigars or 250g of tobacco, and 250ml of perfume.

Health Requirements

A yellow fever certificate may be asked for when entering Zanzibar. Intending visitors should seek medical advice on anti-malarial medication and on other potential tropical diseases well in advance of their trip. Most visitors do not experience serious problems.

Getting There

By Air: Many international airlines now fly directly into Kilimanjaro (Moshi/Arusha) and Julius Nyerere (Dar es Salaam) International Airports. Some flights go through Zanzibar. Some flights go via Zanzibar.

By Road: Frequent luxury buses operate between the Kenyan capital, Nairobi, and Arusha and Moshi in northern Tanzania. Buses also operate between Mombasa and Moshi (northern Tanzania) and Tanga (northern Tanzanian coast). It is also possible to enter Tanzania from Zambia or Malawi.

By Rail: Not advised unless you don't mind discomfort and delays. If you travel first class the long journeys are less arduous though you still have to use the often abysmal toilet facilities.

What to Pack

Lightweight clothing in neutral colours is best in the bush. Long-sleeved shirts and trousers help prevent the mosquitoes biting, and hats, sunglasses and comfortable shoes make life easier and healthier when walking or camping. In the rains an umbrella or light raincoat is handy. Light woollens are needed in highland areas (and sometimes elsewhere in the dry season, from mid-May–mid-October) and heavier clothing at higher altitudes (e.g. Ngorongoro). Those climbing Kilimanjaro or Meru will need layers of warm, waterproof clothing. Strong, comfortable footwear is also needed at higher altitudes.

Evening or city clothes tend to be casual or smart/casual throughout Tanzania.

A **camera** with at least one telephoto lens (200mm and/or above. Most people now use digital cameras so bring spare memory cards and at least one spare battery. If you still use film err on the side of more rather than less; a good pair of **binoculars** (the highest magnification is not always the best factor, and 7 or 8 X 50 is adequate); if you intend to go walking or camping, you might find a small **rucksack** with a torch, penknife and portable water bottle or flask very handy.

Money Matters

Currency: Tanzania has a decimal system based on the Tanzanian shilling (TShs). Notes are in denominations of 500,1,000, 2,000, 5,000 and 10,000 TShs.

Exchange: Foreign currency (cash as well as travellers cheques) may be exchanged at bureaux de change or the larger hotels. It pays to shop around. There is an increasing number of banks, bank branches and ATMs in the main urban areas, so access to your money is usually more straightforward than it once was. The black market has declined considerably but visitors can still expect to be approached by touts – they should be politely turned away.

Banks: The main banks are: Standard Chartered, Barclays, Exim, CRDB, Stanbic Eurafrican and the Bank of

Tanzania. Banking hours are: 08:30 – approx. 12:30 and 13:00–1600 Mon–Fri; 08:30–11:30 Sat; 09:00–11:30 Sun but hours vary from bank to bank.

Credit cards: Most major credit cards are now far more widely accepted than they were a few years ago, but visitors should not take this for granted.

Tipping: Tipping for good service (approx 10%) is always appreciated. A service charge might be included in the bill, but whether this always reaches the appropriate pockets is questionable.

Accommodation

Hotels are graded by a star system but also (especially safari lodges and camps) by the rather ubiquitous use of words such as 'luxury', 'exclusive', etc. Standards have risen in recent years and these days there is a quickly growing number of tourist hotels, lodges and camps to choose from. This guide mentions many of the better ones, but if you are travelling independently it is advisable to consult the Internet.

Transport

Road: Recent rehabilitation of roads has much improved the Tanzanian network. The tarmac highways between Zambia and Dar es Salaam (the Tanzam highway), and Dar and the north are in good condition for most of their length. Elsewhere roads vary from good gravel or dirt tracks to potholed or corrugated trials of

endurance. The situation is improving, and travellers should seek local information before travelling.

Petrol and diesel are readily available along the major tourist routes and in the towns. Independent travellers into the more remote regions, including certain game parks, must be self-sufficient in terms of fuel.

In the event of **breakdowns** on the open road, set up two warning triangles (these are required by law) at appropriate distances either side of the vehicle. If you cannot fix the vehicle yourself, wave down a passing traveller. With locals, discuss payment before accepting help or a tow.

USEFUL PHRASES	
ENGLISH	**SWAHILI**
Hello	Jambo
How are you?	Habari?
Fine/OK	Mzuri
Thank you	Asante
(very much)	(sana)
Welcome!	Karibu!
	(pl. Karibuni)
Excuse me	Samahani
Goodbye	Kwaheri
Yes	Ndiyo
No	Hapana
Today	Leo
Tomorrow	Kesho
Hot	Moto
Cold	Baridi
Hotel	Hoteli
Room	Chumba
Bed	Kitanda
Shop	Duka
One	Moja
Two	Mbili
Three	Tatu
Four	Ine
Five	Tano

There are **garages** in all the large towns. Many of the mechanics are not very thoroughly trained so stay with your vehicle while it is being repaired and make sure you agree on an estimated price before repairs begin.

If you intend driving to remote parts of a particular game park, take a guide or notify the ranger or the manager of your lodge or camp.

Car hire is expensive, but there are an increasing number of options in major towns. Visitors may drive in Tanzania using a valid international driving licence, which should be carried at all times when driving. Driving is on the left. The speed limit on open roads is 80kph (50mph), except where indicated, and in towns 50kph (30mph). There are frequent police checks on major roads, sometimes with radar. Remain patient and calm if stopped.

Bus: Travelling locally on Tanzania's crowded bus services is not advised. Long-distance buses, however,

have improved enormously in recent years, and the best of them are reasonably comfortable and air-conditioned. Routes covered include Dar to Moshi, Tanga to Moshi and Moshi to Arusha. Bus services to Nairobi and Mombasa are also available. Departure times of the main services are usually published in the local press.

Train: There are three major railway lines in Tanzania: Dar–Tanga–Moshi, Dar–Mwanza/Kigoma and Dar–Mbeya–Zambia. Rail travel in Tanzania can be long, uncomfortable and tiring. The 'Uhuru' railway between Dar and Zambia is the most reliable and comfortable of Tanzanian's railways, but first-class travel is advised.

Ferry: The fastest services between Dar and Zanzibar (taking just over one hour) are the hydrofoils run by companies such as Flying Horse and Azam Marine, all of which are based at the customs jetty opposite St Joseph's Cathedral on the main Dar es Salaam seafront.

On Lake Victoria services

run between Mwanza and Bukoba (in Tanzania), and Port Bell in Uganda.

The historical steamer, *M.V. Liemba*, still operates out of Kigoma on Lake Tanganyika, serving Zambia and Burundi.

Air: Air Tanzania, the national airline, is just recovering from a failed merger, but there are now many private airlines offering scheduled flights to all major tourist destinations, as well as charter flights.

Travelling with a Local Safari Company

According to an Internet assessment the top 3 'upper range' safari companies are currently 'Africa Dream Safaris', 'The Exploration Company' and 'Thomson Safaris', the top 3 'mid-range' companies 'Africa Safari Specialists', 'Roys' Safaris' and 'Tropical Breaks' and the top 3 'budget' companies (usually camping) 'Good Earth Tours', 'Pollmans Tours' and 'Wildersun Safaris'. There are, however, many more companies with excellent or very good reputations, including Abercrombie and Kent, Bobby Tours, Bushbuck, Chimpanzee Safaris, Dorobo Safaris, Flycatcher Safaris, Green Footprint Adventures, Ker and Downey Safaris, Leopard Tours, Sunny Safaris, Takim's Holiday Tours and Safaris.

Before finalizing a deal, independent travellers should confirm the main points of the agreement with the company, preferably in writing. Points should include the maximum number of people

CONVERSION CHART

FROM	TO	MULTIPLY BY
Millimetres	Inches	0.0394
Metres	Yards	1.0936
Metres	Feet	3.281
Kilometres	Miles	0.6214
Square kilometres	Square miles	0.386
Hectares	Acres	2.471
Litres	Pints	1.760
Kilograms	Pounds	2.205
Tonnes	Tons	0.984

To convert Celsius to Fahrenheit: x 9 ÷ 5 + 32

per vehicle, your exact itinerary and exactly what the agreement covers (such as game park fees, provision of back-up vehicle in event of major breakdown, etc.)

Business Hours

As a general rule shops open by about 09:00 and close by about 17:00, with a break for lunch from 12:00 until about 15:00. Supermarkets, larger shops and small dukas selling groceries and general goods often stay open all day.

Time Difference

Tanzania has only one time zone, 3 hours ahead of GMT.

Communications

The Tanzanian telephone sytem has improved enormously in recent years. Direct dialing is now widespread and most of the country is covered by cellphone companies such as 'Vodacom', 'Mobitel' and 'Celtel'. Internet facilities and cafés exist in all cities and major towns and many of the smaller ones, as well as in many of the better hotels and lodges.

Electricity

The power system is 220/230 volts AC. US appliances require an adaptor. Plugs are usually 13-amp square pin. Power cuts are fairly common, though most standard tourist hotels and lodges have their own generator.

Weights and Measures

Tanzania operates the metric system.

Health Precautions

Malaria is endemic in all lowland areas below 800m (2600ft) and particularly virulent. Visitors should take prophylactics as prescribed by their doctor. A course of these should begin at least one week before entering the country, and carry on throughout and for two weeks after the stay. In the unlikely event of visitors experiencing any kind of fever on their return home they must seek treatment immediately and inform their doctor of the possiblity of malaria. Measures which can be taken to prevent malaria also include the use of mosquito nets at night, spraying of rooms with insecticide, the application of insect repellant and the wearing of long-sleeved shirts, long trousers, socks and so on in the evenings and early mornings.

Other insect-borne diseases such as **yellow fever** and **sleeping sickness** are present, but for visitors there is little actual fear of contacting most of them. Tsetse flies, one species of which carries sleeping sickness, can give travellers in the bush a sharp little bite, but very few victims actually suffer anything worse than this.

Bilharzia is a debilitating water-borne disease, caused by a parasitical worm, which can be caught by swimming in certain lakes, pools and rivers. Lake Victoria is heavily infested. The disease is easily avoided, by resisting any temptation to swim or wash in such waters.

AIDS is widespread in Tanzania.

Tanzania, especially during and just after the rains, has its share of **creepy crawlies**. Few are threatening, but common sense should be employed. Scorpion, snake and spider bites are very rare and seldom fatal.

On the coast, spiny sea-urchins and stone-fish can cause problems, but they are rarely encountered by tourists. If in doubt, wear strong and thick-soled canvas shoes, and ask for advice at your hotel.

Try to avoid untreated **water**, ice-cubes and raw vegetables, and peel all fruit. Tap water is unsafe for drinking or brushing teeth. Mineral water is available in the larger towns and many restaurants, and most hotels and lodges usually provide flasks of boiled and filtered water (not always to be trusted in salubrious places). Independent travellers should boil or sterilize drinking water and milk.

Cuts, **bites** and **stings** are liable to turn septic if left untreated, so an appropriate ointment should be applied as soon as possible. Cuts and grazes from coral can be particularly easily infected.

Health Services

There are qualified doctors on hand in the major towns, as well as pharmacies selling a wide range of medicines. In the more popular parks many lodges and camps have qualified doctors on hand or on radio call, and in the unlikely event of major accidents or serious illness, patients would be flown out, usually quickly, to an appropriate hospital. Similarly, walkers and climbers on Kilimanjaro can expect fairly efficient medical evacuation in the event of an emergency.

Most travel companies insist on their clients taking out **medical insurance**, but if this is not the case, travellers should make sure that they insure their health before their trip begins.

Security

Petty thieving, thefts of cars and more serious robberies occur in Tanzania, as elsewhere. Care should always be taken of personal property. Don't advertise your

relative wealth and be careful, even when in a car, of wearing jewellery as such items as watches and necklaces are sometimes snatched through open windows. Similarly, beware of pickpockets, and con-men who 'recognize' you from the airport. In the unlikely event of more serious robberies, do not resist.

Drug-related problems, including addiction itself, are on the increase though you are unlikely to encounter unpleasant incidents.

Emergencies

Dial 111,112,999 (fire, ambulance, police).

Etiquette

It is bad mannered to wear revealing clothes especially in Zanzibar or on the coast, except when swimming etc. Shorts, of course, are acceptable in the bush and in most towns with small Muslim populations, especially in tourist areas. When shopping, dealing with taxi drivers etc., haggling is expected, except in supermarkets etc. where of course the prices are fixed. It is considered rude to take photographs of people without asking permission or (having gained permission) agreeing on a fee. Photographing Muslim women without permission is particularly offensive. In no circumstances should photographs be taken of army barracks, trucks police stations, bridges or any other sensitive buildings or areas.

Language

The national language is Swahili, though English is widely spoken in most tourist areas (*see* page 123).

GOOD READING

Brodie, FM, *The Devil Drives* (Eland)
Dugard, Martin, *Into Africa* (Bantam)
Hemingway, Ernest, *Snows of Kilimanjaro* (Random House)
Jeal, Tim, *Stanley* (Faber)
Matthiessen, Peter, *Tree Where Man was Born* (Harvill)
Mercer, Graham, *Bagamoyo, Town of Palms* (available in Dar and Bagamoyo or from gmercer@istafrica.com)
Reader, John, *Africa* (Penguin)
Stanley, HM, *How I Found Livingstone* (White Star Publications.
Stewart, Alexander, *Kilimanjaro, A Complete Trekker's Guide* (Cicerone)

Field guides:
Estes, R *Behaviour Guide to African Mammals* (Russel Friedman).
Estes, R *The Safari Companion* (Russel Friedman).
Kingdon, Jonathan, *Kingdon Pocket Guide to African Mammals* (Russell Friedman)
Richmond, MD *Guide to the Seashores of Eastern Africa* (Sida).
Richmond, MD, *Fieldguide to the Seashores of East Africa* (Dar University).
Roberts *Birds of Southern Africa* (John Voëlcker Bird Book Fund).
Zimmerman/Turner/Pearson *Birds of Kenya and Northern Tanzania* (Helm Field Guides).

INDEX